MEXICAN FLAVORS

MEXICAN FLAVORS

CONTEMPORARY RECIPES
from CAMP SAN MIGUEL

HUGH CARPENTER • TERI SANDISON

Andrews McMeel
Publishing

Kansas City • Sydney • London

JOHN CHADBURN MCDONALD, AKA JOHNNY MAC
SEPTEMBER 17, 1982–OCTOBER 25, 2006
NEPHEW, SON, BROTHER, FRIEND, CHEF
"BON SERVICE"

CONTENTS

THE INDEPENDENCE ROUTE

Our history of San Miguel de Allende begins with the missionary activities of Franciscan Father Juan de San Miguel in 1542 and stretches for centuries along the route from Guanajuato to Mexico City. When Father Juan arrived in this area to build his first "conversion chapel" at San Miguel Viejo, he was hoping to attract the previously nomadic local Indians (called Chicimecas by their more sophisticated peers, the Aztecs who had made their capital south, in Mexico City) and the Otomi Indians. Over several hundred years, many chapels were built for the Indians, mostly along a route that stretches roughly from the great pyramid site (now called Cañada de la Virgen) to the ritual hot springs at Atotonilco, where the Jesuit Father Alfaro (Padre Luis Felipe Neri de Alfaro) built his magnificent church starting in 1740, right on top of the Indians' sacred springs, in hopes that they would join the new faith. Father Alfaro employed a skilled Indian painter called Pocasangre (Antonio Martinez de Pocasangre) to bring the entire New Testament to life through detailed murals on the walls of his glorious edifice. And he finally succeeded in converting many.

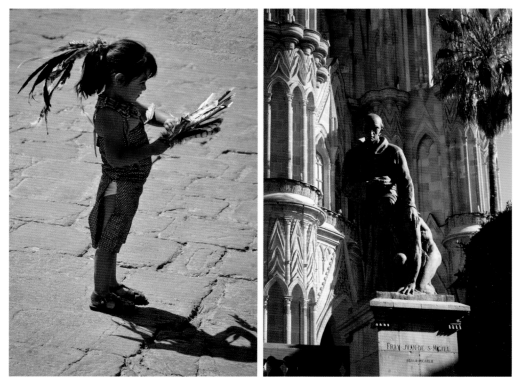

Left, the ritual dances of the Indian cultures are taught to the youngest San Miguel residents. Right, city founder Father Juan de San Miguel's image is still evident in several of the town squares.

During the 1600s, San Miguel had become a successful merchant town serving the silver mining industry, which thrived in the area of Guanajuato. The route, which later would bring independence fighters to battle in Guanajuato, brought the silver traders on the way to Queretero, Mexico City, and beyond to Europe. In the year 1700, 90 percent of the silver mined in the world came from one mine: the Valenciana mine in Guanajuato. The great families of San Miguel, such as the Allendes, the Canals, and the Aldamas, grew and prospered through manufacturing, ranching, commerce, and banking. Their houses can still be visited around the main plaza (*zócalo*) called El Jardin, in front of the landmark church La Parroquia (see page ix).

The colonial government allowed these Spanish-blooded families to prosper, but they could not participate in the highest levels of the colonial government or armed forces if they had not been born in Spain. A huge level of resentment was generated against the overarching colonial government of Spain. The independence movement

had been successful in the United States in 1776, and there were many ongoing movements for self-government throughout Latin America during the early 1800s. In the San Miguel area, an unlikely coalition developed among the terribly overworked laborers, mostly Indians and mestizos (mixed race); their supporters, the Catholic clergy; and the Creoles (criollos, or full-blooded Spaniards born in Mexico).

By the year 1810, centuries of grievances produced a secret conspiracy of independence planners. The clandestine meetings were held at the house of the sub-governor of Queretero and his wife, Josefa Ortiz de Dominguez, in Queretero. Their plan was to attack the Spanish barracks in Guanajuato in October 1810, but word leaked out to the Spanish. An adrenal-charged group of rebel leaders, including General Ignacio Allende and Juan Aldama, gathered the few men they could in San Miguel, and went to Dolores to meet up with their co-conspirator, Father Hidalgo (Padre Miguel Hidalgo y Costillo), a Jesuit priest. On the morning of September 16, 1810, Father Hidalgo made his famous call for liberty, *El Grito*

Left, the Parroquia church in the center of San Miguel. Right, a statue of a leader of the independence movement, Father Hidalgo.

de Dolores (The Cry of Dolores), on the steps of the main church, his church, in the center of town. Then the small group of independence fighters marched on throughout the area to gather men. They stopped at the Church of Atotonilco (Santuario de Atotonilco), where Father Hidalgo grabbed a banner with the image of Our Lady of Guadalupe (Nuestra Señora de Guadalupe), beloved to the common people, who listened to Hidalgo's call for liberty and justice. Hundreds of men joined the ranks in Atotonilco because they had been attending a spiritual retreat there.

This first independence army, mostly on foot and armed with machetes, clubs, slingshots, and bows and arrows, continued to gather fighters. They finally reached the mountainous city of Guanajuato, home of the Valenciana silver mine.

The Spanish soldiers had, of course, been warned of the coming insurrection and had moved with their families into the fortified granary (*alhóndiga*) building in the center of the city. From this strategic location, they were able to fire their rifles from the rooftops down on the freedom fighters. Machetes and rocks were useless weapons in this situation.

A very strong and brave Indian miner, called simply Pipila, strapped a slab of stone onto his back for protection and took a flaming torch up to the great wooden doors of the granary. He successfully ignited the doors, and soon the first legendary battle for independence from Spain was won by the Allende–Hidalgo coalition of insurgents. All of these brave early leaders were eventually killed during the ten long years of the independence movement, but their energy lives on.

We visualize this history when we enjoy a musical performance in the main plaza, El Jardin, in front of the Allende family home; when we drive along the route to Atotonilco to enjoy a gourmet lunch or folk-art shopping; or continue on to Dolores Hidalgo for a few pieces of their famous Talavera-style pottery (an industry founded by the revolutionary priest Father Hidalgo). The legendary figures and places introduced here are still exerting a magnetic presence today along these historic roads.

INTRODUCTION

SAN MIGUEL'S CULINARY LANDSCAPE

Mexican Flavors does for Mexican cooking what our cookbook *Pacific Flavors* did for Asian cuisine. It makes Mexican flavors accessible to American cooks by using everyday American preparation and cooking techniques matched with Mexican ingredients available at American supermarkets. The book provides a road map to re-creating the best flavor memories of Mexico in your kitchen. This is American cooking with a Mexican flair.

Of all the places we have visited in Mexico, San Miguel de Allende has been the most unique. Located high in the mountains north of Mexico City, this colonial town is designated a UNESCO World Heritage Site. In 2013, the readers of *Condé Nast Traveler* called San Miguel "the World's Best City" and described the town with these words: "great atmosphere, excellent restaurants, culture and ambiance galore, romantically and historically beautiful, and an amazing place to be." San Miguel de Allende is known for its art galleries, craft shops, outdoor markets, art and language institutes, fine restaurants, and a large expatriate population drawn from all over the world. It's a town of cobblestone streets, endless holy days, fiestas, vibrant colors, pealing bells, and celebrations.

Traditional snack foods, such as peanuts and corn on the cob, are available from street carts in San Miguel.

Around every corner are exciting taste sensations. Taco stands feature goat, chicken, and pork seasoned with Tomatillo Salsa (page 18). A few steps farther, white crunchy jicama are cut into thick strips and seasoned with lime, ancho chile powder, and cilantro. Why stop eating? There's the famous café specializing in hot chocolate and great Mexican coffee best enjoyed with Mexican doughnuts, or churros, hot from the oil—a sugar-coated and textural marvel. Put on your gastronomic training wheels. Across El Jardin is Restaurant Don Thomas, famous for its version of the classic dish Sopa Azteca (page 91). The soup is a combination of rich tomato broth, thick slabs of avocado, crisp tortilla strips, and a whole chipotle chile floating on the surface.

We've both experienced the magic of Mexico since the 1960s, first as high school and college students crossing Mexico in dilapidated vans, and later on many trips together beginning with an engagement getaway to Oaxaca in April 1985. San Miguel was always on the bucket list. We'd heard the descriptors: "high desert town," "masses of Texans," and "lots of artists"—good for a brief visit, and then we would move onward to more interesting areas. With three other couples from Napa Valley, we arrived late one night in September 2000 for a five-day trip—our first and only visit to San Miguel, that was for certain.

Arriving late at night, the narrow cobblestoned street twisted into the shadows, and a profound stillness concentrated our attention. Through an open entry door, we passed into an ancient colonial fantasy of stone arches, tiled floors, and a rush of tropical plants, home to world-champion ice skater and artist Toller Cranston. Fantastic, alluring, captivating: We couldn't wait to see more after a short sleep. Our trip turned into five nights of parties, five days of exploring up and down the cobblestone streets, in and out of bars and nightclubs. We left no restaurant menu unexplored, no taco stand ignored, and no welcome unannounced to a growing group of new friends seen in El Jardin, at gallery openings, and along the narrow streets. And on day five, just before a rush to the airport, we bought a historic colonial home on Calle Hospicio. So much for escaping the clutches of boring San Miguel.

We entered a new chapter of frequent San Miguel visits after that trip. Buying property in Mexico has a certain Mad Hatter element. The Calle Hospicio purchase was, as it turned out, unrealized, as were several other real-estate deals over the years. Our thoughts turned to our Napa Valley cooking school and to how much fun it would be to share our enthusiasm for San Miguel and our love of Mexican cooking. In 2006, we offered our first six-day program—a mix of cooking classes taught by chefs in their restaurant kitchens and classes taught by us in private homes.

Three years later, bed-and-breakfast owner Dianne Kushner built an event center just outside town. For the next five years, all our cooking programs were held at that property. With its two indoor kitchens, an outdoor kitchen, a vaulted dining room, and a garden pool cascading down the hill, its charm was palpable. Working in cooking teams, with spirits strengthened by the Mexican coffee Café de Olla (page 189) and chilled Cucumber Tea (page 187), we cooked each morning for a couple of hours, followed by lunch using the recipes in this cookbook.

Now we've entered a new chapter in partnership with the deluxe Sierra Nevada Hotel (part of the Orient-Express Hotels). The classes are held in their beautiful cooking school, Sazón, located in a historical colonial building in the heart of San Miguel. With plenty of room for all of us to participate, we barbecue quail (Grilled Quail with Hibiscus Sauce, page 126), roast giant prawns (Cilantro Soup with Prawns, page 97), and make chocolate truffles (Mexican Chocolate Truffles, page 179). The same recipes we teach at Camp San Miguel are found in this cookbook.

Mexican Cooking and Its Food

UNESCO has honored Mexican cuisine with the first-ever award for Intangible Cultural Property. The following is adapted from the United Nations definition of Mexican food:

"Traditional Mexican cuisine is a comprehensive cultural model comprising farming, ritual practices, age-old skills, culinary techniques and ancestral community customs and manners. It is made possible by collective participation in the entire traditional food chain: from planting and harvesting to cooking and eating. The basis of the system is founded on corn, beans, and chiles; unique farming methods such as milpas (rotating swidden fields of corn and other crops) and chinampas (man-made islets in lake areas); cooking processes such as nixtamalization (lime-hulling maize which increases its nutritional value); and singular utensils including grinding stones and stone mortars. Native ingredients such as varieties of tomatoes, squashes, avocados, cocoa, and vanilla augment the basic staples. Mexican cuisine is elaborate and symbol laden, with everyday tortillas and tamales, both made of corn, forming an integral part of festival days throughout the year. Collectives of female cooks and other practitioners devoted to raising crops and traditional cuisine are found across Mexico. Their knowledge and techniques express community identity, reinforce social bonds, and build stronger local, regional, and national identities."

There is no better description of what makes Mexican food "Mexican" than the United Nations summary. The cuisine is diverse. Although Spanish is the common language, there are more than sixty native languages spoken and thousands of unique dishes. Americans' knowledge about Mexican food is largely limited to tacos, enchiladas, chiles rellenos, burritos, guacamole, salsa, and margaritas, which barely begin to represent Mexico's vast recipe collection.

But America's perception of Mexican food is changing. Nearly every American town has a Chipotle Mexican Grill, with its emphasis on fresh ingredients, a menu dominated by guacamole hand-mashed three times a day, and dishes such as carnitas, barbacoa, adobo-marinated grilled steak, and soft tacos. At the other end of the gastronomic spectrum are Rick Bayless (of Topolobampo and Frontera Grill in Chicago), Diana Kennedy and her numerous Mexican cookbooks, and chefs and cookbook authors Roberto Santibanez, Thomas Schnetz, and Scott Linquist, to name a few who are the harbingers of a sophisticated style of Mexican fine dining.

There are many such restaurants now in San Miguel. Owner-chef Donnie Masterton at The Restaurant is continually pushing culinary boundaries. A recent menu included a dish called Chile-Dusted Crispy Shrimp Taco on Jicama Tortilla with Lime and Chile Arbol. Another favorite is his homemade ravioli filled with a local goat cheese in a cilantro butter with toasted walnuts and crispy sage. From this restaurant, it's just a short walk along the narrow cobblestone streets to the ultrasophisticated Hotel Matilda. Here the food is created by the famous Mexico City chef Enrique Olvera. Some of his dishes are Beef Tartar with Serrano Pepper and Goat Buttermilk Crepe; Lamb Empanadas with Molcajete Hot Sauce; and a dessert of Candied Guava Paste with Rice Ice Cream. These examples only scratch the surface of the exciting contemporary food being cooked by Mexican chefs at restaurants across their country.

How to Use This Book

The theme of this cookbook is contemporary. Not every recipe is easy (Pulled Pork with Chiles, Orange, and Cilantro, page 146), and not every recipe is old school (Fusion Empanadas, page 50). The recipes capture the essence of Mexican cooking—its unique flavors.

Mexican food is driven by ingredients. We use the freshest ingredients from local organic growers, dairy farmers, and ranchers to procure the highest quality and most responsibly raised products available. Key ingredients are achiote paste, avocado, beans, chiles, chocolate, cilantro, corn, limes, spices (particularly cinnamon, coriander, and cumin), tomatoes, and tropical fruits. Before you

get started cooking, please read through Chapter 1, Flavor Building Blocks. All special ingredients are defined along with storage information, possible substitutions, and mail-order sources. Nearly all ingredients can be found at typical American supermarkets.

Mexican food is labor-intensive. Traditionally many recipes were prepared with a laborious grinding in a mortar and pestle made from volcanic rock. Electric blenders entered the Mexican kitchen in the 1950s and revolutionized the cuisine. It greatly shortened the preparation time of many dishes, including their famous moles. But some of Mexico's most famous dishes, such as tamales and empanadas, don't appear in this cookbook because of their time-consuming nature. Other recipes, such as the marvelous Chiles Rellenos (page 59), we recommend serving to only a group of four people, because they can be so labor-intensive.

Here are some key things to remember as you dive into the recipes:

1. Read through the recipe completely before beginning.

2. If you have difficulty finding certain ingredients, refer to Chapter 1, Flavor Building Blocks, for easily available substitutes. It is especially important to read the section about chiles and their substitutes on page 6.

3. All recipes give the serving size. Most recipes serve 4 to 6, but an occasional recipe is better made for a larger group, such as Mexican Seafood Risotto (page 116). If doubling a recipe, double all of the ingredients except for the salt, garlic, and chiles. Increase these by 1½ times.

4. All recipes indicate how far in advance the preparation stages can be completed. Many of the recipes can be prepped a day in advance.

In the produce markets, small farmers bring the freshest handpicked ingredients to sell. Here we see chiles and xoconostle, or the fruit of the prickly pear cactus, which is called *nopal* in Spanish.

5. Last, we encourage you to write on the recipes. Make notes, add the date served, to whom you served it, and rank the recipe from 1 to 10, with 10 being perfection. Think of this book as your gastronomic diary. We hope that one day it will find its way to a young cook who shares your passion.

Menu Planning

Don't start your Mexican cooking adventure by planning a dinner party for forty. Begin by preparing and cooking just one Mexican dish and fitting it into an American menu. In this way, you can become comfortable with the Mexican flavor palate, preparation techniques, and cooking procedures. By serving just one Mexican dish as part of the menu, its unique aspects will be celebrated.

Think "we" instead of "I" for a Mexican dinner. Invite a group of cooking friends over and ask each to bring a dish from this book. Delegate and make your Mexican dinner a "we" event.

Use the recipes in this book to inspire trips to trendy Mexican restaurants, whether near your home or in one of Mexico's romantic colonial cities. *Mexican Flavors* provides the kind of recipes we teach at Camp San Miguel. If you can't travel to San Miguel, cooking from this book is the next best thing to being at our side.

Begin the adventure.

—HUGH CARPENTER AND TERI SANDISON
 SAN MIGUEL DE ALLENDE AND
 NAPA VALLEY, 2014

CHAPTER 1

FLAVOR BUILDING BLOCKS

Good cooking begins with great ingredients. This means not only purchasing the freshest vegetables, seafood, meats, and herbs, but also choosing the best types of oils, vinegars, dried chiles, and condiments. In terms of Mexican ingredients, the best are sold at Mexican markets and increasingly are found in the Mexican food aisles of American markets. If you are unsure where the nearest Mexican market is located, ask the owner of your favorite Mexican restaurant for the closest shopping source. All of the ingredients in this chapter can also be mail-ordered from www.mexgrocer.com.

But before proceeding, one of the essential items for Mexican cooking is not a food ingredient at all: It is an electric blender! The blender came to Mexico in the 1950s and was its own revolution. Pre-blender, everything from a simple guacamole to the complex moles had to be pulverized by using a lava rock shaped into a mortar, or a sloping lava stone called a molcajete. You can use a processor instead of a blender. However, the texture of your sauces will be grainier when made in a food processor, and will lack the beautiful, smooth texture that results when using an electric blender. For the best results, use the powerful electric blender made by Vitamix.

About Chiles

Chiles, corn, tomatoes, and chocolate are the four pillars of Mexican cooking. But of these, chiles are the key to the cuisine. Native to the Americas, they have been cultivated for at least a thousand years and were essential in the diets of the Olmecs, Toltecs, Mayans, and Aztecs. Within a hundred years following the arrival of Cortés, the Spanish spread chiles around the globe, transforming the cuisines of far-flung countries.

An understanding of chiles is impossible without *The Great Chile Book* by Mark Miller. This book is an essential resource. It has photographs of all the fresh and dried chiles pictured in their actual size, the spice level of each chile, and the recommended uses and substitutions. We follow Miller's temperature scale, with 10 being the hottest and 1 being the mildest.

FRESH CHILES: Anaheim 2–3, poblano 3, jalapeño 5.5, serrano 7, habanero 10, Scotch bonnet 9–10

Anaheim and poblano chiles are mildly spicy and can be used interchangeably. They have about the same level of spice and are used for many dishes, such as the famous chiles rellenos. These are never eaten raw and are always given a preliminary charring. When dried, poblanos are called ancho chiles (except on the West Coast, where ancho chiles are called pasilla) and Anaheim chiles are called New Mexico chiles (*chile seco del norte*).

Jalapeño and serrano chiles are the two most commonly used fresh chiles in Mexican cooking. Jalapeño chiles vary in spice level, ranging from moderately spicy to mild as a bell pepper. Serranos are hotter, but these, too, vary in intensity. Test the chile by cutting off the stem and tasting the cut surface of the stem for hotness. Adjust the quantity to use accordingly.

JALAPEÑO

SERRANO

HABANERO

ANAHEIM

TO SEED OR NOT TO SEED: When using jalapeño and serrano chiles, never extract the seeds and ribs. Just adjust the hotness of the dish by mincing less of the chile. To mince, use an electric mini chopper. Larger fresh chiles such as poblanos are often seeded first, but there is no hard and fast rule of whether to seed these chiles.

THE PLASTIC BAG TECHNIQUE: Habanero and Scotch bonnet chiles are extremely spicy. When handling these, always protect your hands by placing them inside plastic baggies, or wear food-service plastic gloves. If substituting habanero or Scotch bonnets for serrano chiles: 1 habanero or Scotch bonnet chile = 4 serrano chiles.

HOW TO CHAR FRESH CHILES: All Mexican cooks char fresh chiles by placing them on a thin metal pan called a *comal* that is placed over the highest heat on a gas stovetop. Any heavy frying pan can be substituted for the *comal*. No oil is added to the pan. Or, gripping chiles with tongs, hold the chiles directly over a gas burner turned to high. This can prove frustrating, since the chiles are inclined to fall into or away from the gas flames, which necessitates constant repositioning. This problem can be solved by using a metal-screen cooling rack that is dedicated just to this function. When chiles char on one side, rotate the chiles, and continue charring until blackened on all sides. Don't try to char the chiles on a gas grill or under the broiler. The heat won't be sufficient to blacken the chiles.

POBLANO

TO WASH OR NOT TO WASH OFF THE CHAR? Never wash the chiles to remove the char. Once the chiles are charred on all sides, transfer the chiles to a bowl and cover with plastic wrap. After 5 minutes, rub off the charred bits using dry paper towels. Don't wash the chiles, as this will wash most of the roasted flavor down the drain.

DRIED CHILES

When fresh chiles are dried, their names change. For example, fresh poblano becomes dried ancho, and fresh jalapeño becomes dried chipotle. Size generally determines the spice level. Most dried chiles of the same size have about the same hotness. One exception is ancho chiles and their confusing name. In California, ancho chiles are packaged as pasilla chiles. But in Mexico, ancho chiles are dried poblano chiles, and pasilla chiles are a different chile altogether called chile negro.

The following dried chiles can all be used interchangeably: guajillo 2–4; mulato 2–4; ancho (dried poblano) 3–5; cascabel 4; chile negro (or pasilla) 3–5.

DON'T OBSESS ABOUT FINDING THE CORRECT TYPE OF CHILE:
Chiles of the same size can usually be used interchangeably. But always check the hotness of chiles, both fresh and dried, by having a little taste test and adjusting the amount to be used accordingly.

NEW MEXICO CHILE

TO SEED OR NOT TO SEED THE DRY CHILE BEFORE SUBMERGED IN LIQUID:
Mexican cooks soften dried chiles by submerging them whole in boiling water or chicken broth. Then the softened chiles are stemmed and the seeds rinsed out. But some of the soft, pulpy interior of the chile can be lost this way. A better technique is to snip off the dry stem end and shake out the seeds. Then place the dried chiles in a saucepan or bowl and cover with boiling water or chicken broth. Keep the chiles submerged with a small plate or bowl. Soak for 30 minutes or until softened, (Note that the water or broth does not need to be kept at a simmer or boil. It gradually cools during the soaking process.)

Sometimes dried chiles are too wrinkled to cut them open and shake away the seeds. In that case, just remove the stem and seeds after submerging the chiles.

CASCABEL CHILE

CHIPOTLE CHILE

GUAJILLO CHILE

TO TOAST OR NOT TO TOAST THE DRIED CHILES: Mexican cooks usually give the chiles a preliminary toasting in a hot skillet or pan (*comal*). But if they are toasted for a few seconds too long, the chiles will acquire a bitter taste and the recipe will be ruined. If you skip the preliminary toasting step, the chiles will still give the food a fantastic taste. So, a preliminary toasting of dried chiles is unnecessary.

OTHER CHILE PRODUCTS

CHIPOTLE CHILES IN ADOBO SAUCE: These are smoked jalapeños simmered in a spicy sauce and are typically sold in 4-ounce cans at every Mexican market and many American supermarkets. To use: Finely mince the chiles, including the seeds, and use along with the sauce. Transfer leftovers to a plastic container and refrigerate. Warning: These are extremely spicy.

CHILE POWDER, ANCHO AND CHIPOTLE: These are pure ground chiles, not spice mixes. If you can't locate these products in your local market, they are always available in Mexican markets. You can also make your own by cutting the dried chiles into small pieces and powdering them in an electric spice grinder. Then package, label, and store with your other spices. One ancho chile equals about 2 tablespoons powder.

CHILE SAUCE: This is a general term covering many types of chile sauce, such as Cholula and Tabasco. Or, you can use sriracha, the Asian chili sauce. You can also substitute crushed red pepper, which is sold in the spice section of all markets. It's what appears on the table at all pizza restaurants. This is very spicy, so use sparingly.

ANCHO
(CALLED PASILLA
CHILE IN CALIFORNIA)

Other Ingredients

ACHIOTE PASTE: Mexico's version of a curry paste, achiote paste was originally a Mayan blend of Mexican oregano, cumin, cloves, cinnamon, black pepper, allspice, garlic, and annatto seeds. The latter turns the mixture red. Now achiote paste is sold throughout Mexico and at Mexican markets in this country. It is generally packaged in 3.5-ounce boxes. When buying, always gently press the box to make sure the achiote paste is still soft. If it feels rock-hard, the paste has become stale. We think the best brand is Del Maya.

AVOCADO: This is one of the essential ingredients in Mexican cuisine. Everything depends on the quality of the avocado. Avoid Florida avocados, which have a 6 percent oil content. They don't have the essential buttery taste. And avocados from Chile are picked too underripe. Buy avocados from California and Mexico. These are 30 percent oil, which gives them a wonderful rich mouthfeel and taste. Avocados are extremely sensitive to frost and thus are grown in a very narrow band around the world. There are dozens of varieties of avocado grown in Mexico, ranging from softball-size fruits to ones just slightly larger than your thumb. If you are unsure of the quality of the avocado, buy a couple extra in case the flesh is streaked with gray or brown. Choose avocados that have a slight give when gently pressed with your fingers. If not used that day, then store avocados in the refrigerator, and use them within a few days.

Limes, chiles, ginger, and tomatillos add a lot of "high notes" to Mexican cuisine.

CHICKEN BROTH: While we prefer using homemade chicken stock, all the recipes in this book have been tested using low-sodium chicken broth. Good brands are Kitchen Basics, Swanson, and Imagine.

CHOCOLATE: The only chocolate used in this book is top-quality European or American bittersweet chocolate, such as Valrhona and Scharffen Berger. To use, chip away at the corners using a chef's knife. We dislike Mexican chocolate, such as Ibarra and Abuelito brands, which are grainy and sugary.

CILANTRO: There is no middle ground for this essential herb: People either love it or hate it! What has a wonderful, floral, deep lingering flavor for me tastes "soapy" to others, including Julia Child, who hated the herb. Now scientists have linked the aversion for cilantro with specific genes involved with taste and smell. For those in the anti-cilantro camp, use it in dishes where it is cooked. The cilantro will have a milder flavor. Then try a little sprig of cilantro, raw. Keep trying and be brave. Reeducate those genes! To store, wrap the bunch of cilantro in dry paper towels, then place in a plastic bag and store in your crisper. Wash only what will be used right away. If chopping cilantro, use the whole plant, including all the stems. That is why our recipes call for both cilantro leaves and tender stems.

CINNAMON, MEXICAN: True cinnamon, which is what is used in Mexican cooking, is the papery inner bark of several different species of trees from Sri Lanka. It has hints of sweet, warm, soft citrus notes. American cinnamon is derived from the cassia tree in Vietnam and China. Its bark is coarser, thicker, harder, and has a slightly bitter taste. They can be used interchangeably. Look for jars labeled as Mexican cinnamon in Mexican markets. A good brand is La Morenita.

CITRUS ZEST AND JUICE: For grated citrus zest, use a Microplane, sold at all kitchenware shops. These are 1 by 8-inch thin, flat metal graters. Never buy packaged orange, lemon, or lime juice, which has an inferior taste. Always squeeze your own and use within 4 hours.

COCONUT MILK, UNSWEETENED: Always purchase a brand whose ingredients are just coconut and water. Stir the coconut milk before using. It should have the consistency of whipping cream. Trader Joe's sells a product called Coconut Cream Extra Thick & Rich in 14-ounce cans. This is extremely thick. To use, dilute with an equal amount of cold water. Also appearing in markets are half-gallon containers of a product called coconut milk, which has the consistency of skim milk and lots of additives. Do not buy this product or low-fat coconut milk, which tastes terrible. The best brands: Chaokoh from Thailand and Thai Kitchens. Once opened, refrigerate for no longer than 5 days, or freeze.

CORN: Use fresh corn only at the height of the corn season. It should taste so sweet that the kernels can be eaten raw. Frozen and canned corn is not acceptable as a substitute.

CREMA: This is the Mexican version of sour cream or crème fraîche. It is tarter and thinner than sour cream. It's used as a garnish or topping on many Mexican dishes. Sold in all Mexican markets and now in many American markets, it is easy to make. Take 1 cup whipping cream (pasteurized, not ultra-pasteurized), and stir in 1 tablespoon fresh buttermilk. Transfer to a glass jar, cover loosely with the lid, and place in a warm area, such as above the refrigerator. Leave it for 18 to 24 hours or until it starts to thicken. Stir, tighten the lid, and refrigerate for 12 to 24 hours. Stir well before using. It should be pourable. This keeps for 2 weeks. (This recipe is from the Fine Dining website.) You may substitute sour cream or crème fraîche thinned with whipping cream for crema.

GINGERROOT: These pungent and spicy, knobby brown roots are sold in all supermarkets in the produce section. Buy firm, fresh ginger with smooth skin. Always peel the ginger by scraping off the skin using the edge of a spoon handle, the dull edge of a paring knife, or the ridge on a Chinese bamboo chopstick. Store uncut ginger in the refrigerator or at room temperature for up to 1 month. There is no substitute for fresh ginger. To use, cut the ginger crosswise in paper-thin slices, then mince in an electric mini chopper.

HERBS: Fresh herbs have a far more intense bouquet than their dried siblings. Fresh herbs are available throughout the year at most supermarkets. In an emergency, substitute ½ teaspoon dried herb for 2 tablespoons chopped fresh herbs. For nearly all fresh herbs, separate the leaves from the stems, discard the stems, and then chop or mince the leaves. The exception is cilantro. For minced cilantro, the entire plant is used, including all the stems as well as the leaves.

HIBISCUS FLOWERS: These are reddish-brown dried flowers. Steeped in boiling water, the water becomes a beautiful red with sweet tropical tastes. Hibiscus tea bags are sold in all Asian markets under the name Roselle Tea and at all Mexican markets sold loose or packaged in small plastic bags.

JICAMA: Think of this as a giant round russet potato but with a white, crisp, slightly sweet interior. Covered in a brown skin that hides the white interior, jicama can weigh up to 50 pounds, with the vines growing to 20 feet or longer. Buy only jicama that feels rock hard. Using a sharp knife, cut away the brown skin. The white interior can be cut into various thicknesses, and it is always eaten raw. Trimmed and cut, jicama can be refrigerated for several days without discoloring. What remains of the whole jicama can be wrapped with plastic and also stored in the refrigerator. Discard after 1 week, as by then it will have converted its sugar into starch.

MILK, EVAPORATED AND CONDENSED: Evaporated milk has about 60 percent of the water removed via evaporation. It is then homogenized, fortified with vitamins and stabilizers, and sterilized. Evaporated milk has the same fluid nature as whole milk, but it is slightly darker, with a hint of caramelized flavor. Avoid skim and low-fat varieties. Sweetened condensed milk has had less processing than evaporated milk. It contains 40 to 45 percent more sugar, and it is pasteurized during the evaporation procedure. It is very thick, almost syrupy. Evaporated milk and condensed milk cannot be used interchangeably. We prefer Carnation brand for condensed milk.

OIL: "Flavorless cooking oil" means any tasteless oil that has a high smoking temperature. The best types are grape-seed oil, rice bran oil, and peanut oil. Canola oil, safflower oil, and corn oil are acceptable alternatives.

OREGANO, MEXICAN: Mexican oregano and Mediterranean oregano are from two entirely different plants. Mediterranean oregano is a member of the mint family, sometimes called wild marjoram. Mexican oregano is a relative of lemon verbena and is native to Mexico. It is similar in taste to Mediterranean oregano but with added notes of citrus and licorice. More aggressive in flavor, it is a perfect match for Mexican dishes.

OYSTER SAUCE: Also called oyster-flavored sauce, this gives dishes a rich taste without a hint of its seafood origins. It is used by innovative Mexican chefs for fusion Mexican dishes. There really is no substitute. It keeps for up to 6 months in the refrigerator. The best brands are Sa Cheng, Hop Sing Lung, and Lee Kum Kee, Old Brand.

PEPPERCORNS, TRICOLOR: Sold in the spice rack of every supermarket, these are a mix of black, white, pink, and green peppercorns. To use, grind in a spice grinder or in a pepper grinder.

PILONCILLO: This is Mexican raw sugar sold in a cone shape of varying sizes. You may see it labeled in America as panela sugar, though this term is not used in Mexico. It has a marvelous caramel-molasses flavor. It keeps indefinitely at room temperature. You may substitute dark brown sugar.

POMEGRANATE MOLASSES (OR SYRUP): This is a dark brown–colored liquid with a syrupy consistency and a wonderful sweet-tart, fruity taste. It's great used on pancakes, in salad dressings, and to rub on fish about to come off the grill. It's available at Middle Eastern markets, fine-food shops, and large supermarkets. There is no substitute.

PUMPKIN SEEDS, PEPITAS: One of the three earliest plants domesticated in the Western Hemisphere along with corn and common beans, called "The Three Sisters," pepitas, or pumpkin seeds, are sold both whole and hulled. When sold whole, they are flat oval, white seeds. Do not buy these. Instead, buy pepitas hulled. Hulled pepitas look small, almost the size of a pine nut, and have a green tint. To use, toast them in a dry skillet over medium heat. When they begin to brown and start to pop, slide them immediately out of the pan and let cool to room temperature. They will keep for up to 6 months stored in a plastic resealable bag in the freezer.

QUESO FRESCO: Traditionally, this "fresh cheese" is made from raw cow's milk or a combination of cow's and goat's milks. It is salty and crumbly and is very similar to soft goat cheese or low-salt feta, both of which can be used as a substitute. In Mexico, this cheese is made fresh every day. The store-bought variety will keep, refrigerated, for 2 weeks.

SESAME SEEDS, WHITE: Buy white sesame seeds sold in the spice section of every American supermarket. Avoid brown or toasted sesame seeds, which are inferior in flavor.

SOY SAUCE: "Thin" or "light" soy sauce is a mildly salty liquid made from soybeans, roasted wheat, yeast, and salt. This is not to be confused with low-sodium soy sauce, which is an inferior-tasting product. The best brands are Pearl River Bridge Golden Label Superior, Koon Chun thin soy sauce, or Kikkoman regular soy sauce. "Dark" or "mushroom" soy sauce is thick enough to coat the neck of the bottle and is far more flavorful than "thin" soy. It is used to darken sauces. The best brand is Pearl River Bridge mushroom soy.

SPICES: Referring to any part of the dried plant except the leaves, this category includes roots (ginger, turmeric, wasabi), bark (cinnamon), berries (allspice), seeds (coriander), seedpods (cardamom), and dried flower buds (cloves). The most common spices used in Mexican cooking are cinnamon, cumin, coriander, and peppercorns. Grind the spices in an electric spice grinder. The spice will have a more intensely fresh flavor than the pre-ground spices sold in the supermarket spice section.

TEQUILA: This is a distilled drink made from the blue agave plant near Guadalajara and the highlands of the western state of Jalisco. To learn more, see page 182.

TOMATILLOS: Pale green, very firm, and about the size and shape of a lime, these are one of the basic building blocks of Mexican cuisine. Slightly sour, with hints of apple, they are used in many green salsas and sauces. Tomatillos, like the tomato, belong to the nightshade family. Look for tomatillos whose papery husk is tightly clinging. The tomatillos should be very firm and the surface of it under the husk will feel slightly sticky. Don't try to wash off the stickiness. Often a part of the tomatillo exterior will have a purplish coloration. This is fine, but do not buy any tomatillos that are even the slightest bit soft. Prior to use, the paper husk is always removed. Then for most recipes the tomatillos are given a browning in a very hot, dry skillet. Cook until there are a few brown spots here and there and the tomatillo is heated through, about 2 minutes. (You are not trying to blacken the exterior like charring a pepper.) Extra tomatillos can be stored in a paper bag and refrigerated for up to 1 month.

TOMATOES: Native to the Americas and spread throughout the world by the Spanish, the tomato is an essential ingredient in Mexican cooking. Any dish using tomatoes will either triumph or sink to a wretched level based on the quality of the tomatoes. Use only vine-ripened tomatoes, which are available from May through October. Avoid all canned or boxed tomatoes when possible.

TORTILLAS, CORN AND FLOUR: These are essential to Mexican cuisine. Used as a wrap to hold cooked foods, or fried into chips, or powdered for mole sauces, good-quality corn and flour tortillas are available at many American markets. Flour tortillas are used mostly in northern Mexico, which is the wheat-growing area, while corn tortillas are used in the central and southern parts of the country. When buying, select the thinnest tortillas. Gently bend each package. The tortillas that bend the easiest are the freshest. To warm in the microwave, wrap 8 tortillas in a damp paper towel. Microwave on High power for 60 seconds. To warm in the oven, wrap 10 tortillas in a damp paper towel, then wrap in aluminum foil, and heat in a 325°F oven for 20 minutes. To warm on the grill or gas stovetop, place the tortillas over direct fire for a few seconds on each side. (If you have an electric stove, use a dry frying pan over medium heat.) To keep warm, wrap tortillas in a warm, damp napkin and place in a basket or a terra-cotta tortilla warmer.

VANILLA BEAN PASTE: Sold in small jars at gourmet markets, this is a thick vanilla syrup with little specks of vanilla bean particles suspended throughout. In recipes using vanilla extract, substitute an equal amount of vanilla bean paste. The flavor will be superior.

WORCESTERSHIRE SAUCE: This is used a lot by Mexican cooks. As a good substitute, replace it with an equal amount of thin soy sauce or oyster sauce.

CHAPTER 2

CORE RECIPES

GUACAMOLE

MAKES 2 TO 3 CUPS

Guacamole, margaritas, and salsa; For Americans, no other dishes so epitomize Mexican cuisine. And no other recipe is easier to make than guacamole—or to put it another way, is easier to ruin. Everything depends on the quality of avocado. A rock-hard avocado shipped thousands of miles from Chile is a sham, a pale pretender to the throne. Great guac starts with avocados from Mexico or from the Southern California coast. Check the label, then gently press the avocado. When perfectly ripe, there should be a slight give. As children, we were always told that placing the avocado pit on top of the guacamole prevents discoloration. This is a myth except for the guacamole lying just underneath the seed! To prevent discoloration, always stir in lime juice, and press plastic wrap directly across the exposed surface. Refrigerated, guacamole will keep its bright color for several days. Great guacamole should have a little texture, so avoid the food processor and just mash the avocado with the tongs of a fork. And please don't turn guacamole into a sort of "garbage" dish by adding all sorts of extras such as chopped tomato, celery, or oddities such as sliced grapes. It's the buttery avocado taste and texture that should dominate. Last, great guacamole depends on having the perfect level of salt. We always enlist dinner guests to help us do a taste test, and there is never a shortage of volunteers!

3 ripe avocados

2 whole green onions, chopped

2 cloves garlic, minced

1 serrano chile, minced, including the seeds

2 tablespoons chopped fresh cilantro, leaves and tender stems (optional)

Freshly squeezed juice of 2 limes

½ teaspoon salt

Cut the avocados in half and remove the pits. With a spoon, scoop out the flesh. Then mash the avocados with the tongs of a fork. Stir the avocados together with the green onions, garlic, chile, cilantro, lime juice, and salt in a medium bowl. Taste and adjust the seasonings for salt, lime juice, and chile.

If making this more than 1 hour in advance, squeeze a little lime juice over the surface, then press plastic wrap directly across the surface of the guacamole. The guacamole will stay perfectly green for 2 days stored this way in the refrigerator.

Variation
Garnish with crumbled goat cheese, queso fresco, or crema.

SALSA MEXICANA
MAKES 4 ½ CUPS

Only make this when vine-ripened tomatoes are available. The tomatoes are chopped by hand, including the skin and seeds. This takes time, but using a food processor gives the salsa an unappealing mushy texture.

4 cups chopped vine-ripened tomatoes, including skins and seeds

¼ to ½ cup coarsely chopped fresh cilantro, leaves and tender stems

2 whole green onions, minced

1 to 2 serrano chiles, minced, including the seeds

3 cloves garlic, minced

½ teaspoon salt

In a large bowl, combine the chopped tomatoes with the cilantro, green onions, chiles, garlic, and salt. Taste and adjust the seasonings, especially for salt and chile flavor. This can be made 3 days ahead and kept refrigerated in an airtight container. Bring to room temperature before serving.

Option
When vine-ripened tomatoes are unavailable, we have used hot house tomatoes and added 1 tablespoon tomato paste (from a tube, not canned) and 2 tablespoons Chinese oyster sauce.

TOMATILLO SALSA

MAKES 2½ CUPS

The green salsa served in every Mexican restaurant is made from the slightly sour tomatillo, a close relative to the tomato. For more information about tomatillos, see page 13. In this salsa, the roasted poblano chile deepens and lengthens the flavor of the salsa. An excellent variation is the addition of a finely diced avocado, used in place of or in addition to the poblano.

8 small green tomatillos, husks removed

1 poblano chile

3 cloves garlic, peeled

1 serrano chile

¼ cup packed fresh cilantro, leaves and tender stems

½ teaspoon salt

In a dry, heavy frying pan over medium-high heat, lightly char the tomatillos. (It's impossible to brown the tomatillos on all sides. Just brown them on the tops and bottoms and on a few places on their sides.) Char the poblano and rub off the blackened skin as described on page 125. Then discard the seeds and stem. Cut the tomatillos into quarters. In the same dry, heavy frying pan over high heat, lightly brown the garlic and serrano chile. Cut the garlic and chiles a few times so they are in slightly smaller pieces.

Place the poblano chile, tomatillos, garlic, serrano-garlic mixture (including the seeds), cilantro, and salt in a blender. Blend until smooth. Alternatively, if you have the time, finely chop the salsa ingredients by hand for a more interesting texture. Taste and adjust the seasonings for salt. This can be stored for 3 days refrigerated in an airtight container. Bring to room temperature before serving.

Freshly picked tomatillos.

BANANA SALSA *with* FOUR VARIATIONS

MAKES 2 CUPS

There is the element of surprise when serving banana salsa. Dinner guests look at this as odd and nibble at the edges suspiciously. Then in an instant, no more banana salsa remains. It's great served as an appetizer with chips, with any meat or seafood entrée coming off the grill, or even eaten secretly spoonful after spoonful.

2 firm yellow skinned bananas

1 red bell pepper, stemmed and seeded

1 whole green onion, minced

¼ cup chopped fresh cilantro, leaves and tender stems

2 tablespoons minced fresh ginger

1 serrano chile, finely minced, including the seeds

3 tablespoons freshly squeezed lime juice

2 tablespoons light brown sugar

½ teaspoon salt

Peel the bananas and cut lengthwise into long strips. Cut across the strips so that the banana is in ½-inch cubes. Mince the red bell pepper and green onion.

Combine the bananas with the bell pepper, green onion, cilantro, ginger, chile, lime juice, brown sugar, and salt in a medium bowl. Press plastic wrap directly across the surface. The salsa can be made 12 hours in advance of serving and kept refrigerated in an airtight container. Bring to room temperature and stir before serving.

Variations

MANGO SALSA
Replace the bananas with 3 perfectly ripe mangoes. Cut away the skin of the mangoes. Cut off the flesh in large pieces, and then chop coarsely to yield 2 to 3 cups. Combine the mango with the remaining ingredients as directed.

PAPAYA SALSA
Replace the bananas with 2 firm, underripe Hawaiian papayas or a 3-inch-thick slice of Mexican papaya. Peel, seed, and chop the fruit to yield 2 to 3 cups. Combine the papaya with the remaining ingredients as directed.

TROPICAL SALSA
Replace the bananas with a mix of chopped fruits—avocado, papaya or mango, strawberries, and kiwi—to yield 2 to 3 cups. Combine the mixed fruit with the remaining ingredients as directed.

PINEAPPLE SALSA
Replace the bananas with 2 to 3 cups chopped fresh pineapple. Omit the lime juice. Combine the pineapple with the remaining ingredients as directed.

TANGERINE-SERRANO SALSA

MAKES 3 TO 4 CUPS

Don't try this with orange segments, but wait until tangerines are in season. The salsa will have a much better taste and texture.

1 tablespoon finely grated tangerine zest

4 tangerines, peeled, segments separated and chopped

½ cup chopped red onion

¼ cup chopped fresh cilantro, leaves and tender stems

1 serrano chile, minced, including the seeds

3 cloves garlic, minced

2 tablespoons minced fresh ginger

¼ cup freshly squeezed lime juice

¼ cup lightly packed light brown sugar

½ teaspoon salt

Combine the tangerine zest and segments, onion, cilantro, chile, garlic, ginger, lime juice, brown sugar, and salt in a medium bowl. This can be made 24 hours in advance and kept refrigerated in an airtight container. Bring to room temperature before serving.

Brightly flowering vines fit in with the colorful palette of house paints.

WATERMELON RELISH

MAKES 3 CUPS

It's the contrast between the watermelon reduction with its spicy seasonings and the refreshing crunchy cubes of watermelon that makes this relish a visual and textural treat. Serve at room temperature, spooned on meats and seafood just removed from the grill. Garnish with crumbled queso fresco or a drizzle of crema.

3 pounds seedless red watermelon

2 tablespoons minced fresh ginger

½ serrano chile, minced, including the seeds

¼ cup freshly squeezed lime juice

¼ cup lightly packed light brown sugar

½ teaspoon salt

2 tablespoons chopped fresh cilantro, leaves and tender stems

2 tablespoons chopped fresh mint leaves

Remove all the rind from the melon and cut the melon into ½-inch cubes. You should have about 6 cups. Place 4 cups of the watermelon in a blender. Add the ginger, chile, lime juice, brown sugar, and salt. Blend until liquefied. Transfer to a large saucepan. Bring to a rapid boil over medium-high heat and boil until reduced to 1 cup. Transfer to a bowl and let cool to room temperature.

Stir in the remaining 2 cups chopped watermelon, the cilantro, and mint. This can be made 2 days ahead and kept refrigerated in an airtight container. Serve at room temperature.

MEXICAN CHILE SAUCE
MAKES 3 CUPS

This sauce can be spooned over grilled meat, or spread on each dinner plate, topped with grilled meat, and garnished with avocado slices. It can also be spooned into martini glasses with three large chilled cooked shrimp nestled inside. Garnish the sauce with crema and then start plunging the shrimp into the sauce.

1½ ounces guajillo chiles, about 6

2 large vine-ripened tomatoes, 12 to 16 ounces

4 cloves garlic, peeled

1 serrano chile

¼ cup lightly packed light brown sugar

½ teaspoon ground cumin

1 teaspoon dried oregano, or 2 teaspoons minced fresh oregano, preferably Mexican

½ teaspoon salt

Cut the stem ends off the guajillo chiles and shake out the seeds. Place the guajillos in a bowl and cover with boiling water (put a small plate on top of the chiles to submerge them). Soak for 30 minutes, then drain, reserving 1 cup of the chile soaking water.

Cut the stems off the tomatoes and slice them in half horizontally. Place a dry cast-iron frying pan over medium-high heat. When hot, lightly brown the garlic, tomatoes, and serrano chile, 5 minutes. Discard the tomato skins.

In a blender, add the guajillo chiles, garlic, tomato, serrano, brown sugar, cumin, oregano, salt, and the 1 cup reserved chile water. Blend until liquefied. Taste and adjust the seasonings. This will keep refrigerated for 3 months stored in an airtight container.

There are still a number of horses in the city center. Young tourists can have their photos taken on this gentle beast.

ANCHO CHILE JAM

MAKES 2½ CUPS

This recipe was given to us in 1992 by Houston chef Robert Del Grande. It has a sweet, slightly spicy, complex flavor, with hints of plum from the ancho chiles. We swirl it into soups, or float little lettuce cups on the soup with Ancho Chile Jam balanced on the lettuce. It's also great used as a chutney next to meat hot off the grill or rubbed on meat or seafood just before grilling. Or you can also make a zigzag garnishing sauce by combining the jam with mayonnaise or Mexican crema.

2 ounces ancho chiles, about 5

2 cloves garlic, peeled

6 tablespoons any kind of red jam or jelly

2 tablespoons honey

2 tablespoons white or red wine vinegar

½ teaspoon salt

Using scissors, cut the ancho chiles open, discard the stems, and shake out all the seeds. Place the chiles in a bowl and add enough boiling water to cover the chiles. Place a small plate on top of the chiles to submerge them. Soak for 30 minutes, then drain, reserving 1 cup of the chile soaking water.

Place the chiles, garlic, jam, honey, vinegar, and salt in a blender. Add the 1 cup reserved chile soaking water and blend on high speed for 1 minute. Transfer the jam to an airtight container and refrigerate for up to 6 months.

In addition to providing security, walls and doors impart a sense of mystery about the patios and gardens they hide.

THREE DRY RUBS

These dry rubs are great on any meat that can be grilled or oven-roasted. Each rub makes about 6 tablespoons, enough to season 8 of your favorite steaks, or 8 chicken breasts, or 3 pounds of fish. Just rub the dry rub into the surface of the meat or seafood, then rub the meat with extra-virgin olive oil. As another option, after rubbing the meat with the dry rub, we like to rub the meat with Chinese mushroom soy sauce or Chinese dark soy sauce. This is not authentic Mexican, but it is delicious! Remember, the rub has to be massaged with vigor into the meat fibers. Then when you brush the meat with a marinade or olive oil before cooking, the rub will not dislodge from the meat during grilling.

DRY RUB #1

MAKES ABOUT 6 TABLESPOONS

1 tablespoon salt

1 tablespoon crushed red pepper

1 tablespoon coriander seeds

1 tablespoon cumin seeds

1 tablespoon caraway seeds

1 teaspoon whole cloves

1 (1-inch) cinnamon stick, preferably Mexican

Place all of the ingredients in a clean electric coffee grinder or spice grinder. Grind into a fine powder. Transfer to an empty glass spice jar, label, and store in your spice rack for up to 6 months.

DRY RUB #2

MAKES ABOUT 6 TABLESPOONS

1 tablespoon salt

1 tablespoon curry powder

1 tablespoon crushed red pepper

1 tablespoon rainbow peppercorn mix

1 tablespoon coriander seeds

1 tablespoon espresso powder

Place all of the ingredients in a clean electric coffee grinder or spice grinder. Grind into a fine powder. Transfer to an empty glass spice jar, label, and store in your spice rack for up to 6 months.

The well-stocked kitchen pantry of the Rancho Cooking School.

DRY RUB #3

MAKES ABOUT 6 TABLESPOONS

¼ cup lightly packed light brown sugar

1 tablespoon ancho or
chipotle chile powder

1 tablespoon coriander seeds

1 (2-inch) cinnamon stick,
preferably Mexican

Place all of the ingredients in a clean electric coffee grinder or spice grinder. Grind into a fine powder. Transfer to an empty glass spice jar, label, and store in your spice rack for up to 6 months.

ALL-PURPOSE MARINADE FOR CHICKEN, PORK, and SEAFOOD

MAKES ½ CUP

Be sure to rub the seasonings into the meat or seafood before adding the olive oil. Done in this manner, the seasonings will stay embedded throughout the cooking process. You can marinate the meat or seafood this way for up to 2 hours before cooking. This marinade makes enough to use on the same quantity of protein as described in the headnote for Three Dry Rubs (page 26).

1 tablespoon freshly ground black pepper

2 teaspoons finely grated lime zest

2 teaspoons finely grated orange zest

1 teaspoon ground coriander or cumin

1 teaspoon ground cinnamon, preferably Mexican

½ teaspoon salt

¼ cup extra-virgin olive oil

Combine the pepper, zests, coriander, cinnamon, and salt in a small bowl. Rub the spice blend over the surface of the meat or seafood. Next, rub the olive oil over the entire surface as well. Proceed with grilling or roasting, as desired.

Many types of beans are sold in the produce markets, such as these fresh garbanzos, left, and dried beans, right, for refried bean recipes (frijoles).

REFRIED BEANS

MAKES 2 CUPS

Refried beans are such a staple of Mexican cuisine that they make an appearance on nearly all plates for breakfast, lunch, and dinner. It's only fancy Mexican restaurants that eschew refried beans. Use them as another flavor/texture element served with any of the entrées in this book. Add the refried beans as one of the layers when creating your own tacos and tostados. And serve them whenever you are making eggs for breakfast. But no matter how you serve them, for great-tasting refried beans, lard is the essential ingredient. It's the lard that gives the refried beans a more rounded taste and a richer flavor that lingers longer on the tongue than when using something "healthy" such as sunflower oil, corn oil, or olive oil. How bad is lard? Lard has more monounsaturated fats ("good" fats) than sunflower oil and corn oil. It has more polyunsaturated fats (also "good" fats) than olive oil. Lard has 30 percent less saturated fat than butter. And lard has no trans fats at all. So for the sake of your health, don't wait. Make this recipe today—with lard!

1 cup dried black beans

3 tablespoons lard

1 medium yellow onion, diced

2 cloves garlic, minced

½ teaspoon salt

Spread the beans on a plate and pick through the beans to remove any pebbles. Rinse the beans, then cover with cold water and soak overnight.

Drain the beans and add to a saucepan. Add 4 cups hot water to the soaked beans. Simmer over medium heat until tender, about 1½ hours. Remove and reserve 2 cups of the cooking water. Alternatively, follow the quick-cooking directions on the bean package.

In a large frying pan, melt the lard over medium heat. Add the onion and cook until the onion becomes golden, about 10 minutes. Add the garlic and cook for 1 more minute. Add the salt and beans. Mash the beans with a fork, adding just enough of the reserved cooking water to make the beans smooth. Alternatively, place in a food processor and process until smooth. The beans can be made up to 4 days in advance. Let cool and then refrigerate in an airtight container.

THREE ZIGZAG SAUCES

Here are three sensational Mexican sauces that can be used in a multitude of ways. Use these to flavor chilled shrimp or to add flavor and a color boost to meat or seafood just taken off the grill. Add a new and exciting taste to chilled smoked salmon or roasted vegetables. Enhance just-cooked panfried dumplings with these or use when "building" tacos and tostados. Experiment!

CHIPOTLE CHILE ZIGZAG SAUCE

MAKES ¾ CUP

½ cup crema, mayonnaise, or sour cream

1 chipotle chile in adobo sauce, minced

1 clove garlic, minced

2 teaspoons finely grated lime zest

1 tablespoon freshly squeezed lime juice

¼ teaspoon salt

Combine all of the ingredients together in a small bowl or an electric mini-chop. Keep refrigerated in an airtight container and use within 1 week.

CILANTRO ZIGZAG SAUCE

MAKES ¾ CUP

½ cup crema, mayonnaise, or sour cream

½ cup fresh cilantro, leaves and tender stems

1 tablespoon finely minced fresh ginger

1 tablespoon freshly squeezed lime juice

¼ teaspoon salt

Combine all of the ingredients together in a small bowl or an electric mini-chop. Keep refrigerated in an airtight container and use within 1 week.

ORANGE-GINGER ZIGZAG SAUCE

MAKES 1 CUP

½ cup crema, mayonnaise, or sour cream

1 tablespoon Grand Marnier

1 tablespoon freshly squeezed lime juice

2 teaspoons Worcestershire sauce

2 tablespoons chopped fresh mint leaves
or cilantro leaves and tender stems

2 tablespoons minced fresh ginger

1 clove garlic, minced

½ serrano chile, minced,
including the seeds

½ teaspoon finely grated orange zest

½ teaspoon salt

Combine all of the ingredients together in a small bowl or an electric mini-chop. Keep refrigerated in an airtight container and use within 1 week.

The dining room at Camp San Miguel, set up for a festive lunch.

CHAPTER 3

APPETIZERS
Set the Stage: The Opening Act

GRAVLAX INFUSED *with* CHILES, CILANTRO, AND TEQUILA

SERVES 8 TO 12

This recipe adds a Mexican twist to a Scandinavian classic by replacing vodka, fresh dill, and ground black pepper with tequila, chopped cilantro, and fresh chiles. To serve this for a Saturday night dinner party, begin curing the salmon on Thursday. The key is salting and weighting the fish. The salt pulls the moisture from the fish, while the weight pressing down on the salmon gives the fish a firm, dense texture. Curing a smaller amount of salmon than this is impractical. If serving this to a small group, the unused cured salmon will keep in the refrigerator for 3 days. Use it for sandwiches, snacks, salads, and more appetizers.

TEQUILA MARINADE

1 cup inexpensive tequila

4 serrano chiles, minced, including the seeds

½ cup chopped fresh cilantro, leaves and tender stems

¼ cup minced fresh ginger

2 tablespoons sugar

2 tablespoons salt

1 teaspoon ground cinnamon, preferably Mexican

∽

1 pound fresh center-cut salmon fillet, skin and pinbones removed

FINISHING SAUCE

½ cup mayonnaise

1 tablespoon freshly squeezed lime juice

2 teaspoons Worcestershire sauce

2 tablespoons chopped fresh cilantro, tender leaves and stems

1 serrano chile, minced, including the seeds

1 tablespoon minced fresh ginger

2 teaspoons finely grated orange zest

½ teaspoon salt

∽

30 water crackers or 1 hothouse cucumber, for serving

2 tablespoons chopped fresh cilantro, leaves and tender stems, or parsley

To make the tequila marinade, combine all of the ingredients in a small bowl. Place the salmon and the marinade in a resealable plastic bag. Securely close the bag, place on a tray, and refrigerate. Then place a 5-quart pot filled with cold water on the salmon. Refrigerate for 2 to 3 days. It is unnecessary to turn the salmon.

Within 2 hours of serving, remove the salmon from the refrigerator. With a wet hand, wipe the marinade off the salmon on both sides. Very thinly slice the salmon into about 30 pieces. Press a piece of plastic wrap across the top so that the slices do not dry out, and refrigerate until ready to serve.

To make the finishing sauce, combine all of the ingredients in a small bowl. Stir well.

If serving with cucumber, cut the cucumber crosswise into 30 thin slices, each about ⅛ inch thick. To serve, place the salmon on the crackers or sliced cucumber. Top with the sauce and garnish with the cilantro. Serve within 30 minutes.

Ritual dances of the Indian cultures are performed at the beginning of every Catholic procession as well as special feast days.

SALMON *and* SCALLOP CEVICHE

SERVES 6 TO 10

It's important to use flawlessly fresh fish here. The fish is "cooked" by soaking in a lime juice bath for 3 hours. It is then tossed with extra-virgin olive oil, serrano chiles, and other seasonings. Placed on a little guacamole at the fat end of endive leaves, this recipe is a colorful, flavorful, textural marvel. You can substitute other fish, such as tuna, swordfish, and sea bass. For presentation variations, serve the ceviche on rice crackers, tortilla chips, or thinly sliced hothouse cucumber.

¼ cup extra-virgin olive oil

1 tablespoon minced fresh ginger

1 clove garlic, minced

1 serrano chile, minced, including the seeds

3 to 4 tablespoons chopped fresh cilantro, leaves and tender stems

1 small whole green onion, minced

¼ cup chopped red bell pepper

1 teaspoon freshly grated nutmeg

½ teaspoon salt

¼ pound fresh salmon fillet, skinned and pinbones removed

¼ pound fresh bay scallops or fresh sea scallops, thinly sliced

½ cup freshly squeezed lime juice

½ cup Guacamole (page 16)

16 endive leaves

Combine the olive oil, ginger, garlic, chile, cilantro, green onion, red bell pepper, nutmeg, and salt in a covered airtight bowl and refrigerate. This can be completed 8 hours before serving and kept refrigerated.

Cut the salmon crosswise into ¼-inch slices; then cut across the slices to make ¼-inch pieces. Mound the scallops together and cut into thin slices—these do not have to be all the same size. Place the salmon and scallops in a medium bowl. Cover with the lime juice and refrigerate for 3 hours. To serve, drain the salmon and scallops. Stir the seafood into the ginger-cilantro mixture until evenly combined. Place about 1 teaspoon of the guacamole at the fat end of each endive leaf. Add a spoonful of the ceviche. Arrange on a serving platter and refrigerate. This can be done 2 hours before serving.

MARINATED GOAT CHEESE *with* CHILES AND MINT

SERVES 8 TO 12

It's the infused oil that gives this goat cheese an intense and exciting flavor. The marinated goat cheese is also very good used as a filling for the center stalks of celery, on taco chips, or with your favorite rice crackers. In terms of technique, since goat cheese tears easily, cut the goat cheese with dental floss rather than with a knife.

1 (12-ounce) log soft goat cheese, about 1 inch in diameter, chilled

1 serrano chile, minced, including the seeds

3 cloves garlic, minced

½ cup slivered fresh mint leaves or chopped cilantro leaves and tender stems

1 teaspoon finely grated orange zest

¾ cup extra-virgin olive oil

1 tablespoon tricolor peppercorns

1 teaspoon allspice berries

½ teaspoon ancho or chipotle chile powder (optional)

30 of your favorite crackers or Belgian endive leaves, for serving

Using dental floss, cut the goat cheese into ½-inch-thick slices. Place the slices in a single layer in a glass baking dish.

In a small bowl, combine the serrano chile, garlic, mint, and orange zest. In a 10-inch sauté pan, combine the oil, peppercorns, and allspice. Place the sauté pan over medium-high heat and cook until the peppercorns begin to pop, about 2 minutes. Turn off the heat and immediately stir in the garlic mixture. After 5 seconds of stirring, pour the hot oil mixture over the cheese. You can prepare the dish to this point up to 3 days before serving and keep it refrigerated in an airtight container.

To serve, transfer the cheese to a serving plate. Spoon some of the infused oil that has pooled around the goat cheese over the top of the goat cheese. Sprinkle the chile powder, if using, over the top. Serve at room temperature with the crackers or endive leaves.

SUMMER ROLLS *with* APPLES AND CHIPOTLE

SERVES 4 TO 8

This recipe uses Vietnamese rice paper as a wrap that is filled with rich-tasting avocado, tropical papaya, crisp apple, and crunchy cucumbers. The rolling of these can be a little taxing, so we make this recipe only when we know some of our dinner guests will be willing to lend a hand. A glass of wine helps speed the process, too. The summer rolls taste delicious dipped in any of the salsas in Chapter 2.

1 ripe avocado

1 Hawaiian papaya or 1 (2-inch) slice underripe Mexican papaya

1 tart apple, such as Pink Lady or Fuji

2 pickling cucumbers or Japanese cucumbers

16 (6½-inch) sheets rice paper wrappers, such as Flying Horse brand

½ cup cilantro sprigs

Chipotle or ancho chile powder

Your choice of salsa, for serving (see pages 17–20)

Cut the avocado in half and remove the pit. Cut each half into 8 long slices. Peel and remove the seeds from the papaya. Cut the papaya into ⅛-inch-thick slices. Then overlap the slices and cut into matchstick pieces. Stem and core the apple. Cut the apple into ⅛-inch-thick slices. Overlap the apple slices and cut into matchstick pieces. Cut the cucumbers on a sharp diagonal into ⅛-inch-thick slices. Overlap the slices and cut into matchstick pieces. In a medium bowl, combine the papaya, apple, and cucumbers. Gently toss to evenly combine.

Dip 2 sheets of rice paper for 10 seconds into a bowl of very hot water. Lay the 2 sheets side by side on the counter. For each rice paper, add 1 slice avocado, ¼ cup of the papaya mixture, 1 cilantro sprig, and a generous sprinkling of chile powder. Turn the wrapper sides over the filling, and then roll into a compact cylinder. Place on a damp towel and cover with a damp towel. You can refrigerate the rolls for up to 3 hours prior to serving. Prepare a salsa.

When ready to serve, center the bowl of salsa on a round or oval serving dish. Place the rolls (not stacked or touching each other, or they'll stick) around the salsa. Or serve individually on small plates with the salsa.

SEARED TUNA *with* TROPICAL SALSA

SERVES 6 TO 10

Buy only the finest-quality tuna, bright red and glistening, for this recipe. It's given a brief searing on a blazing-hot cast-iron skillet, then cut into thin slices and placed on rounds of cucumber. Or, it can be served balanced on taco chips or in endive cups. Don't try cooking the tuna on a gas or charcoal grill. By the time the exterior becomes lightly charred, the interior of the tuna will be overcooked.

1 pound sushi-grade tuna
steak, 1 inch thick

2 teaspoons freshly ground black pepper

½ teaspoon salt

4 teaspoons extra-virgin olive oil

1 teaspoon finely grated lime zest

1 teaspoon finely grated orange zest

1 tablespoon flavorless cooking oil

Tropical Salsa, for serving (page 19)

1 hothouse cucumber

Cut the tuna into log-shaped pieces, about 1 inch square and 4 inches long. Rub the tuna on all sides with the pepper, salt, olive oil, and lime and orange zests.

Heat a cast-iron frying pan over high heat until very hot, about 3 minutes. When very hot, brush with the cooking oil, then immediately add the tuna. Sear the tuna for 15 seconds on each side, for a total cooking time of 1 minute. The tuna should be raw to rare in the center. Transfer to a cutting board, and cut the tuna into twenty ¼-inch-thick slices. This can be done 4 hours ahead; refrigerate the tuna in an airtight container. Make the Tropical Salsa.

To assemble, cut the cucumber crosswise into twenty ⅛-inch-thick slices. Place a single layer of cucumber slices on a serving platter. Add 1 slice of tuna on top of each cucumber slice. Top each with a little salsa.

The younger generation enjoys learning the Indian dances and traditions.

CHILLED SHRIMP *with* SMOKED TOMATO RELISH

SERVES 8 TO 12

Chilled shrimp and a rich tomato relish are nestled together here in martini glasses. The relish is also very good spooned over meat or fish just removed from the grill or oven. It's also excellent without the shrimp and poured into shooter or tequila glasses and served chilled as an appetizer on its own.

1½ pounds (13–15 count) raw extra-large shrimp, shells on

5 large vine-ripened tomatoes, about 1½ pounds

2 tablespoons granulated sugar

¼ cup lightly packed light brown sugar

¼ cup red or white wine vinegar

2 tablespoons Worcestershire sauce

1-2 chipotle chiles in adobo sauce

2 tablespoons minced fresh ginger

2 cloves garlic, minced

½ teaspoon salt

¼ cup crumbled queso fresco or crema

2 tablespoons chopped fresh cilantro, leaves and tender stems

Prepare an ice water bath in a large bowl. Bring 4 quarts of water in a large pot to a vigorous boil over high heat. Add the shrimp and cook for exactly 3 minutes. Immediately transfer the shrimp to the ice water and submerge. Chill for 5 minutes. Peel the shrimp, leaving the tails on. Cut along the top ridge and devein. Refrigerate in an airtight container until ready to use within 24 hours.

Prepare a hot fire in a gas or charcoal grill. With a serrated knife, slice off and discard the tomato tops and bottoms. Cut the tomatoes in half horizontally. Sprinkle both sides with the granulated sugar. When the grill is very hot, transfer the tomato slices to the grill. Grill until charred on the underside, about 5 minutes. Turn the tomatoes over, cover, and char for 3 more minutes. Remove from the grill and let cool slightly.

Discard the tomato skins and place the tomatoes in a blender. Add the brown sugar, vinegar, Worcestershire, chipotle, ginger, garlic, and salt. Blend to a smooth consistency. Transfer the tomato mixture to a medium saucepan. Boil on medium-high heat until thick, about 4 minutes. You will have about 2 cups. Remove from the stove and refrigerate. This can be done 24 hours in advance; refrigerate the relish in an airtight container.

To assemble, pour the chilled relish into 6 to 8 martini glasses. Place 3 chilled shrimp in each glass. Just before serving, garnish with the crumbled queso fresco and the chopped cilantro.

BBQ SHRIMP PACKED *with* SERRANO-HERB BUTTER

SERVES 6 TO 10

First the shrimp shells are snipped open along the top ridge. Then a spicy garlic butter is rubbed between the shells and shrimp. In this manner the Serrano-Herb Butter stays trapped between the shell and shrimp, adding a profoundly intense taste as each shrimp is peeled and eaten. If you don't want to serve the shrimp shell-on, you can peel them. If you do, melt the herb butter in a saucepan. Just before grilling the shrimp, toss the raw shrimp with the melted butter. Then grill the shrimp, brushing on more melted butter during cooking. But beware of flame-ups!

2 pounds large to jumbo raw shrimp, shells on

4 cloves garlic, peeled

3 serrano chiles

½ cup packed fresh cilantro, leaves and tender stems

Finely grated zest of 2 limes

½ teaspoon salt

1 cup butter, cut into 8 pieces, at room temperature

2 limes, cut into wedges

Using scissors, cut along the top ridge of each of the shrimp shells. Devein without dislodging the shells.

Using a food processor, mince the garlic. Stem the chiles and cut into small pieces. With the machine running, drop the chiles into the food processor with the garlic. When minced, add the cilantro and mince again. Add the lime zest, salt, and butter to the food processor, and run the machine until all becomes a smooth mix.

Place the herb butter underneath the shrimp shells by putting a little herb butter on your index finger and then smearing the butter under the shell. The butter does not have to be under the entire shell, just a little bit on each side of the shrimp. This can be completed up to 12 hours ahead; refrigerate the shrimp in an airtight container.

Prepare a medium-hot fire in a gas or charcoal grill. To cook the shrimp, place the shrimp on the grill, and cook until the shells blacken and the shrimp are cooked through, turning them over several times (to test for doneness, cut into the shrimp). Serve with the lime wedges.

QUESADILLAS *with* PAPAYA AND BRIE

SERVES 6 TO 10

This is a very easy and utterly delicious appetizer with a real flavor explosion. Of course, Brie is not authentically Mexican, but the taste is sublime and it melts beautifully. Buy an inexpensive firm Brie. Quesadillas taste best when cooked in a frying pan with a little butter. But they can also be toasted on the grill until heated through. Use a pizza cutter to divide the quesadillas into wedges. For more texture, sprinkle ¼ cup chopped jicama across the surface of each quesadilla.

About 4 ounces not-quite-ripe papaya

4 ounces firm Brie

4 (10-inch) flour tortillas

½ cup Mexican Chile Sauce (page 22) or taco sauce

1 cup Guacamole (page 16)

2 whole green onions, minced

¼ cup chopped fresh cilantro, leaves and tender stems

1 tablespoon unsalted butter

Peel, seed, and very thinly slice the papaya. Cut the Brie into very thin pieces, including the rind.

Place the tortillas on the counter. Spread 2 tortillas with the chile sauce (¼ cup for each tortilla), and the other 2 tortillas with the guacamole. On top of the sauce, add even layers of the papaya, Brie, green onions, and cilantro. Cover with the other tortillas (guacamole side down) and press firmly. This can be completed up to 2 hours before; refrigerate the quesadillas.

To cook the quesadillas, place a 12-inch sauté pan over medium-high heat. When hot, add 1½ teaspoons of the butter. When the butter melts and becomes light golden, add 1 quesadilla. Spin the quesadilla a few times to evenly distribute the butter. Cook until golden, about 30 seconds, then turn the quesadilla over and cook on its second side until golden, about 30 seconds.

Transfer the quesadilla to a plate. Cover with a dry kitchen towel to keep warm. Add the remaining 1½ teaspoons butter and cook the second quesadilla in the same way. Cut the quesadillas into wedges and serve.

SPICY SMOKED BABY BACK RIBLETS

SERVES 4 TO 8

These ribs are coated with a spicy, complex sauce. By having the butcher cut the rack in half horizontally to produce 2 equal strips of ribs, they are easy to cut, serve, and consume! The ribs are also great served as an entrée, accompanied by Yellow Watermelon Salad (page 77), Mexican Garlic Bread (page 156), and large servings of Coconut Ice Cream (page 169). Your dinner guests will never want to leave!

3 to 5 chipotle chiles in adobo sauce

8 cloves garlic, minced

¼ cup minced fresh ginger

2 whole green onions, chopped

2 teaspoons ground coriander

1 teaspoon ground cumin

1 (1-inch) cinnamon stick, preferably Mexican

1 teaspoon salt

1 rack pork back ribs, silverskin removed by your butcher and ribs cut in half horizontally

¼ cup extra-virgin olive oil

⅓ cup crema

¼ cup chopped fresh cilantro, leaves and tender stems

Mince the chipotle chiles and combine them with the garlic, ginger, and green onions in a small bowl. In a clean electric spice grinder, combine the coriander, cumin, cinnamon, and salt. Grind to a powder. Rub both sides of the ribs with the chipotle mixture. Then rub the meat vigorously with the spices. Last, rub the ribs with the olive oil. The ribs can be marinated up to 8 hours in advance and stored covered in the refrigerator.

To cook, bring the ribs to room temperature if necessary. Prepare a low fire in a charcoal or gas grill (about 300°F). Place the ribs in a rib rack and position the rib rack over indirect heat. Alternatively, lay the ribs meaty side up directly on the cooking grate, positioned away from the heat. Cover the grill and cook the ribs until the meat has begun to shrink away from the ends of the bones, about 1½ hours. (Try to maintain the heat around 300°F.)

Cut each rack into riblets and transfer to a platter. Drizzle the ribs with the crema and sprinkle with the chopped cilantro.

Note: The ribs can be kept warm for 1 hour by placing the ribs in a sealed thick paper bag on the kitchen counter. Or cook ahead, refrigerate, and then warm in a 250°F oven, covered, for 30 minutes.

GUACAMOLE PIZZA

SERVES 4 TO 8

Many years ago, Napa Valley chef Richard Haake was making pizzas at our home. Always on the search for new techniques, we lurked around, observing him. With a few quick motions, he layered the pizza dough thickly with guacamole and then slid the pizza into a 1,000°F pizza oven. Insane—what a sure way to ruin guacamole! It would obviously turn black from the heat. A hush fell over our dinner guests. And then suddenly there was the pizza, beautifully crisp and covered with brilliantly green guacamole. With a deft sprinkling of crumbled goat cheese and chopped roasted red pepper, the pizza was soon missing in action as dinner guests set to work fulfilling their duties. Here is what Richard achieved.

PIZZA DOUGH

¾ cup warm water

2 teaspoons active dry yeast

1 teaspoon sugar

3 tablespoons extra-virgin olive oil, plus a little extra

1 teaspoon salt

2 cups unbleached all-purpose flour, bread flour, or "double 00" flour

∽

Guacamole (page 16)

2 tablespoons extra-virgin olive oil

4 ounces queso fresco or goat cheese, crumbled

½ cup roasted red pepper, chopped

To make the dough, combine the water, yeast, and sugar in a glass measuring cup. When a little foam forms on the surface, stir in 2 tablespoons of the olive oil and the salt. Measure the flour into a large bowl. Stir in the yeast mixture until the dough comes together. Knead until no longer sticky, about 5 minutes. Lightly coat the dough with the remaining 1 tablespoon olive oil. Place in a bowl and cover with a towel. Let rise at room temperature until it doubles in size, about 1 hour. Divide the dough in half. (You will need only 1 half for this recipe; place the other half in a resealable plastic bag and refrigerate or freeze for another time.) The dough can be made 1 day ahead and refrigerated.

To make the pizza, place a pizza stone on the bottom rack of the oven. Turn the oven to 525°F or the highest temperature setting and preheat for 45 minutes. Stretch the pizza dough into a very thin circle. Place the pizza dough on a wooden pizza paddle (best) or use a piece of cardboard (works OK) or the underside of a baking pan that is well floured. Spread a thick layer of the guacamole across the dough, edge to edge. Brush the edge of the pizza with the olive oil. Slide the pizza off the paddle onto the heated pizza stone. Cook until the crust becomes golden, about 12 minutes.

Remove the pizza from the oven and sprinkle with the queso fresco and chopped red pepper. Cut into wedges and serve at once.

WINGS *with* JALAPEÑO GLAZE

SERVES 6 TO 12

When cooking chicken wings, there is no better cooking technique than slow-roasting them. During the long cooking, the marinade caramelizes into a deep mahogany glaze. It's difficult to stop eating these sticky, sweet, and spicy wings. Very versatile, they are great hot out of the oven, at room temperature, or gently reheated in a 300°F oven for 20 minutes. If you are unable to find jalapeño jam, substitute any jam or jelly (try raspberry, apple, currant, or mango), and stir in 3 minced jalapeño chiles.

1 teaspoon salt

2 teaspoons freshly ground black pepper

2 teaspoons ground cumin

1 cup red or green jalapeño jam

1 cup spicy taco sauce

½ cup thin soy sauce

½ cup freshly squeezed lime juice

2 jalapeño chiles, minced including seeds

6 cloves garlic, minced

¼ cup chopped fresh cilantro, leaves and tender stems

24 chicken wings

In a bowl, combine the salt, pepper, cumin, jam, taco sauce, soy, lime juice, chiles, garlic, and cilantro. Makes 3 cups. In a bowl large enough to hold the wings, combine the wings and jam mixture. Cover and marinate the wings in the refrigerator for 1 to 24 hours (the longer they marinate, the better they will taste).

To cook the wings, preheat the oven to 375°F. Line a shallow baking pan with aluminum foil. Coat a wire rack with nonstick cooking spray and place the rack in the baking pan. Drain the chicken and reserve the marinade. Arrange the wings on the rack, smooth skin side down. Roast for 30 minutes. Drain the accumulated liquid from the pan. Baste the wings with the reserved marinade, turn them over, and baste again. Roast 15 minutes. Baste only the top surface. Roast another 15 minutes (1 hour total roasting time). Cut the wings in half through the joint. Serve hot or at room temperature.

SALMON SATAY *with* ZIGZAG SAUCE

SERVES 4 TO 8

The key to this recipe is to cut the salmon into thick enough pieces so that when you run each skewer through each salmon piece, only the bamboo tip and the handle are visible. In other words, err on the side of thicker versus thinner pieces. No guest is going to say, "Oh, the salmon's too thick!" If you want to avoid the last-minute cooking tribulations, grill the salmon skewers shortly before the dinner guests arrive. The satay tastes just as delicious at room temperature. In place of the salmon, substitute boneless, skinless chicken thighs or beef tenderloin.

1 pound center-cut salmon fillet, skin and pinbones removed

2 cloves garlic, minced

¼ cup lightly packed light brown sugar

1 teaspoon ground cumin

1 teaspoon salt

Freshly ground black pepper

¼ cup extra-virgin olive oil

16 bamboo skewers, 6 inches long

One of the Zigzag Sauces (page 30)

Cut the salmon into ⅓-inch-thick pieces, each 1 to 2 inches long. Combine the garlic, brown sugar, cumin, salt, and black pepper in a small bowl. Rub this on both sides of each piece of salmon. Rub the salmon all over with the olive oil. Then slide a bamboo skewer through each piece lengthwise, stopping when the bamboo tip is barely visible. This can be done 1 day in advance of cooking and kept refrigerated in an airtight container.

Prepare a medium-hot fire in a gas or charcoal grill.

To cook the salmon, brush the cooking grate with vegetable oil. Place a double layer of aluminum foil along the front of the cooking grate. Add the skewers so the salmon is directly over the heat but the foil is under the exposed bamboo skewers. Grill the salmon, turning several times, for about 4 minutes total. Depending on the size of the grill, you may need to do the cooking in 2 batches. Transfer to a platter.

Put the Zigzag Sauce into a resealable plastic bag and cut off the corner. Gently squeeze the bag, making a zigzag pattern across the salmon skewers. Serve hot or at room temperature.

SHRIMP DUMPLINGS *with* CHILE CREAM SAUCE

SERVES 8 TO 12

What would a Chinese chef marooned in Mexico City create? Here is the answer! This recipe gives rise to many variations. Try substituting raw salmon fillet or ground meat such as ground lamb, pork, or veal for the shrimp. However, ground chicken and turkey are not good choices here, as their low fat content results in an unpleasantly dry texture.

¾ pound raw shrimp, peeled and minced

1 tablespoon minced fresh ginger

2 whole green onions, minced

1 tablespoon oyster sauce

30 to 36 (3½-inch) very thin wonton wrappers

Cornstarch, for dusting

½ cup low-sodium chicken broth

¼ cup heavy cream

1 vine-ripened tomato, minced

2 tablespoons chipotle chiles in adobo sauce, minced

1 tablespoon oyster sauce, or ½ teaspoon salt

1 tablespoon chopped fresh cilantro, leaves and tender stems, or basil leaves

2 tablespoons flavorless cooking oil

Combine the shrimp, ginger, green onions, and oyster sauce in a bowl. Mix well using your fingers. Trim the wonton wrappers into circles, if necessary. Fold the dumplings. Place about 2 teaspoons shrimp filling in the center of each wonton skin. Draw the wonton skin up around the sides of the filling. Gently squeeze the waist of the dumpling with your thumb and forefinger while you flatten the top and bottom of the dumpling using your other hand. Each dumpling should look like a column with a flat bottom. You should have enough filling for 30 to 36 dumplings. Place the finished dumplings on parchment paper that is lightly dusted with cornstarch. The dumplings can be refrigerated uncovered (no plastic wrapping used) for up to 12 hours in advance.

To make the cream sauce, combine the chicken broth, cream, tomato, chipotle chiles, oyster sauce, and cilantro in a bowl. Refrigerate until ready to serve.

To cook the dumplings, place a 12-inch nonstick sauté pan over high heat. Add the cooking oil and immediately add the dumplings, flat side down. Fry the dumplings until the bottoms become dark golden, about 2 minutes. Pour in the cream sauce. Immediately cover the pan, decrease the heat to medium-high, and cook the dumplings until they become firm to the touch, about 30 seconds. Remove the lid and shake the pan so that the dumplings "capsize" and are glazed on all sides with the sauce. Tip out onto a heated serving platter and serve at once.

FUSION EMPANADAS

SERVES 8

Empanadas are half-moon-shaped pastries stuffed with meat or seafood. They are common not only in Mexico but also throughout Latin America. This recipe is made easier by replacing the pastry dough with wonton wrappers. The result is a light, crisp "fusion" empanada that is sensational as an appetizer.

PORK FILLING

½ pound ground pork

2 whole green onions, minced

¼ cup chopped fresh cilantro, leaves and tender stems

1 tablespoon Mexican Chile Sauce (page 22) or Chinese chile sauce

2 cloves garlic, minced

½ beaten egg

½ teaspoon salt

Cornstarch, for dusting

20 to 24 (3½-inch) round wonton wrappers

3 tablespoons flavorless cooking oil

Zigzag Sauce of your choice, for serving (page 30)

To make the pork filling, combine the ground pork, green onions, cilantro, chile sauce, garlic, egg, and salt in a medium bowl. Using your hands, mix the ingredients until evenly blended. This can be made 24 hours in advance and kept refrigerated in an airtight container.

To wrap the empanadas, first prepare a small bowl of water. Line a baking sheet with parchment paper and dust it with cornstarch. Place a round wonton wrapper on a flat surface. Add about 1 tablespoon of the pork filling, forming it lengthwise. Dip your fingers into the water and then gently moisten the wonton around the filling. Fold the wrapper over the filling, and pinch the outside edges to seal into a half-moon shape. Place the empanadas on the baking sheet. This can be done 12 hours in advance; refrigerate the empanadas. Prepare the Zigzag Sauce. Place in a resealable plastic bag and cut one corner off the bag.

To cook the empanadas, place a 12-inch nonstick sauté pan over high heat. Add the cooking oil. Add the empanadas (they should all fit in the pan). Cook until brown on the bottom side, then turn over each empanada (use 2 spoons to do this) and brown on the other side. Add ¼ cup water. Cover the sauté pan tightly. Cook for about 20 seconds. Remove the lid—the empanada skins should be transparent, and they are cooked when the filling feels firm when prodded with a finger. Boil away the remaining water. Slide the empanadas onto a serving platter.

Squeeze the Zigzag Sauce in a random zigzag pattern over the empanadas. Serve at once.

MEATBALLS *with* BLACK PEPPER, SERRANO, AND HOT SAUCE

SERVES 8

This is a very easy hot appetizer that has a wonderful blend of flavors. The meatballs can be formed a day in advance, placed on a shallow baking pan, and refrigerated. Then once the dinner guests assemble, crowding into the kitchen to see what you have been up to, the meatballs are popped into a hot oven for 3 to 4 minutes. Topped with a little guacamole and a zigzag of crema, they will disappear within moments. You can use ground beef, veal, or lamb, but we prefer lamb because of its rich taste. If you use ground beef, buy beef that is at least 20 percent fat, which provides more flavor.

½ pound ground beef, ground veal, or ground lamb

1 large egg, lightly beaten

1 tablespoon Worcestershire sauce

1 tablespoon Mexican hot sauce (such as Cholula)

1 whole green onion, minced

1 clove garlic, finely minced

1 serrano chile, minced, including the seeds

1 tablespoon chopped fresh oregano, preferably Mexican (or cilantro or mint)

1 tablespoon minced fresh ginger

1 teaspoon freshly ground black pepper

½ teaspoon ground cumin

¼ teaspoon salt

½ cup unseasoned bread crumbs

About ½ cup Guacamole (page 16)

¼ cup crema

In a bowl, combine the beef with the egg, Worcestershire sauce, hot sauce, green onion, garlic, chile, oregano, ginger, pepper, cumin, and salt. Using your hands, mix well.

Place the bread crumbs on a plate. Lightly oil your hands with flavorless cooking oil or olive oil. Then form the meat into compact little meatballs, making 16. Coat on all sides with the bread crumbs. Transfer the meatballs to the baking pan. This can be done 24 hours in advance; refrigerate the meatballs in an airtight container.

Line a 9 by 13-inch pan with aluminum foil. Add the meatballs.

To cook the meatballs, preheat the oven to 400°F. When the oven has been preheated, turn the oven setting to broil. Place the baking pan in the oven 4 inches below the broiler. Cook the meatballs for 3 to 4 minutes; they should be lightly browned and feel slightly soft when prodded with a finger.

Transfer the meatballs to a serving plate. Add about a teaspoon of the guacamole on top of each meatball. Drizzle the meatballs with the crema and serve at once.

FOUR BELOVED COUNTRY FOODS

Tacos, Tostadas, Chiles Rellenos, and Enchiladas

TACO AND TOSTADA
CREATIONS

*T*acos are flour or corn tortillas filled with enchanting layers of cold and hot ingredients, then formed into a loose cylinder and eaten using your hands. Messy, satisfying, and delicious, these creations are available on many street corners of San Miguel, often from vendors who operate only during the evening hours.

Tostados are flour or corn tortillas that are first given a brief frying in oil until crisp and then served open-faced. Tostados are flat tacos and use the same layering of ingredients as tacos. They are eaten with a knife and fork. To fry the tortillas, place 2 cups flavorless cooking oil in a 12-inch frying pan. Heat until the edge of a tortilla dipped into the oil begins to bubble. Fry the tortillas, one at a time, until golden and crisp, about 1 minute. Drain and pat dry with paper towels to remove any extra oil.

Here are the basic building blocks. It's not necessary to utilize all six layers for every taco or tostado! For example, you might choose a taco using just a layer of guacamole, then baby arugula, then grilled fish. There are two recipes that follow as examples. Now you're free to create new combinations.

First Layer: A little smear of Guacamole (page 16), Ancho Chile Jam (page 23), or Mexican Chile Sauce (page 22).

Second Layer: Shredded iceberg lettuce or any salad mix.

Third Layer: Meat or seafood sliced into thin pieces. This can be meat or seafood grilled or roasted. We especially like using meat or seafood placed on skewers and grilled (see page 48).

Fourth Layer: Coleslaw for moisture and texture.

Fifth Layer: A couple of spoonfuls of salsa or your favorite hot sauce.

Sixth Layer: Optional drizzle of one of the Zigzag Sauces (page 30)

BBQ CHICKEN TACOS *or* TOSTADOS

MAKES 8 TACOS OR TOSTADOS

A soft chicken taco wrapped around a supermarket roast chicken, avocado slices, and a store-bought salsa makes a satisfying weeknight dinner. But the following recipe, with its sophisticated taste and texture mix, is great for informal dinner parties. We serve this as the only appetizer, and often it is the only Mexican-inspired dish on the menu. Or, it's great as the main course, accompanied by a Caesar salad. An ambitious cook might grill jumbo shrimp or skirt steak alongside the chicken thighs, and add a few salsas from pages 17–20, to create a greater variety of Mexican flavor options.

1 pound boneless, skinless chicken thighs

2 tablespoons dry rub of choice (see page 26)

3 tablespoons extra-virgin olive oil

8 (6-inch) corn or flour tortillas

Flavorless cooking oil (if making tostados)

Guacamole (page 16)

2 cups shredded iceberg lettuce

Coleslaw Dressing (page 73)

Your choice of salsa (see pages 17–20)

½ cup crumbled queso fresco or crema

Prepare a medium-hot fire in a gas or charcoal grill. Cut the chicken into 1 ½-inch-wide strips. Rub with the dry rub, and then with the olive oil. Grill the chicken for 3 minutes on each side. Let cool, then thinly slice the chicken.

Warm the tortillas as directed on page 13. Then transfer to a basket lined with a cloth towel, and wrap the tortillas to keep warm.

For tacos, all the elements can be served at the table with everyone building their own. Or (more work and not as much fun), they can be assembled in the kitchen, and the tacos placed on a serving platter or dinner plates.

If making tostados, heat ½ inch cooking oil in a deep frying pan to 375°F. The end of a tortilla strip should bubble when dipped into the oil. Fry the tortillas until crisp. Drain on paper towels, and then place flat on serving plates. Then add the layers on top of the tortillas: first guacamole, then lettuce, chicken, coleslaw, salsa, and cheese.

BBQ SEA BASS TACOS OR TOSTADOS
with LIMES, CHILES, AND GUACAMOLE

MAKES 8 TACOS OR TOSTADOS

Is there any other dish than fish tacos that captures the heart of Mexican cooking? Perfectly cooked fresh fish, the crisp coolness of shredded iceberg lettuce, the richness of ripe Hass avocado, and the sparkling fresh flavors of salsa, all wrapped in a warm charred tortilla, recalls lingering memories of Mexican taco stands along their beautiful beaches.

1½ pounds fresh sea bass, skinned (or any firm fish)

Dry Rub for Meat or Seafood (page 26)

3 tablespoons extra virgin olive oil

8 (6-inch) flour tortillas

¼ cup Ancho Chile Jam (page 23)

3 cups baby arugula or shredded iceberg lettuce

Pineapple Salsa (page 19)

Guacamole (page 16)

Chipotle Chile Zigzag Sauce (page 30)

2 limes, cut into wedges

Flavorless cooking oil (if making tostados)

Prepare the Dry Rub, ancho chili jam, salsa, guacamole, and Zigzag Sauce.

Prepare a medium-hot fire in a gas or charcoal grill. Place a layer of aluminum foil over the grill grate. Rub the sea bass with the rub then with olive oil. Grill the sea bass on the foil for 8 minutes with the grill covered. Check the fish. If it does not begin to flake, cover the grill and cook for 2 more minutes.

If making tacos, warm the tortillas as directed on page 13. Add a little smear of ancho chile jam. Add some arugula, fish, and a spoonful of the salsa. Add a little guacamole, and top with a drizzle of the zigzag sauce. Serve at once, accompanied by the lime wedges.

If making tostados, heat ½ inch cooking oil in a deep frying pan to 375°F. The end of a tortilla strip should bubble when dipped into the oil. Fry the tortillas until crisp. Drain on paper towels and then place flat on serving plates. Add all the layers as described above. Serve at once.

CHILES RELLENOS
THREE FILLINGS AND
THREE COOKING METHODS

This is a time-consuming but grand-tasting recipe. For this reason, involve your cooking friends to help stuff and cook the rellenos. You'll have more fun doing it together. If you are not serving the rellenos as the main course, then be sure that the other dishes require no last-minute cooking. You can make the filling and stuff the chiles 24 hours in advance of serving. The actual cooking of the stuffed chiles is a last-minute activity.

The Chiles: Poblano chiles are commonly used, but the long, slender Anaheim chiles are also good. Buy poblanos that are evenly shaped with no indentations. Char and skin the chiles as described on page 125. Be careful not to over-char! There should still be small amounts of the shiny green surface visible. After rubbing off the skin, make a slit lengthwise along each chile. Do not remove the seeds or wash the chiles. If you are going to shallow fry the chiles, it is very important that the chiles are bone-dry inside or else there is the potential during frying of a terrible explosion of water and hot oil.

The Filling: A large poblano holds ½ to ¾ cup filling. An Anaheim or small poblano holds ½ cup or a bit less filling. Due to the short cooking time of the chiles, all seafood and meat must already be precooked. Since each of the filling recipes here makes 2 cups, if you want to serve the chiles rellenos as a main course, you will probably want to double the filling recipe.

Closing the Stuffed Chiles: It is unnecessary to close the chiles using toothpicks or kitchen string. The goat cheese acts as a binder and prevents the chile from opening during the cooking.

The Batter: Stuffed chiles that are deep-fried need to be encased in a protective batter. Bring the chiles to room temperature. Just before cooking, using an electric beater, beat 3 egg whites until stiff. Add ½ teaspoon salt. With the mixer on, beat in 3 egg yolks. The batter is a Diana Kennedy technique. Transfer the batter to a 9 by 9-inch pyrex baking dish.

The Frying Method: If you are cooking more than 4 chiles, use 2 frying pans. Place a 12-inch frying pan(s) over high heat. You can do this on the stove, or place the frying pan(s) over high heat on an outdoor gas grill. Pour 3 cups flavorless cooking oil into each pan. Wait until the oil gets hot enough so that the end of a wooden spoon dipped into the oil begins to bubble around the tip. Coat the chiles with white flour. Then, holding the chiles by the stem, twirl them in the batter until well coated. Holding one chile by the stem, place a clean fork under the tip of the chile, and coat the chile with batter. Then lay the battered chile in the hot oil (do not rush—be careful). Fry until golden on all sides and the chile becomes hot in the center, about 5 minutes total cooking time. Transfer to dinner plates, or if cooking two batches, temporarily place on a wire rack. When cooked, serve immediately.

Hugh Carpenter demonstrating the frying of Chiles Rellenos.

The Roasting Method: This method is for unbattered chiles. Bring the chiles to room temperature. Place the chiles on a wire rack and place in a preheated 350°F oven. Roast until thoroughly heated, about 20 minutes.

The Barbecue Method: This method is for unbattered chiles. Bring the chiles to room temperature. Prepare a medium-hot fire in a gas or charcoal grill. You'll need a double layer of aluminum foil, about 12 by 12 inches, with one side sprayed with nonstick cooking spray. Place the foil over direct heat with the oiled side up. Place the stuffed chiles on the foil. Cover the grill. Cook until the chiles are piping hot, about 15 minutes. To add more flavor, place 2 cups of hardwood chips directly on the fire before beginning to cook. When the chips begin to smoke, place the chiles on the foil and cover the grill.

Serving: Make 1 chile per person as a first course and 2 chiles per person as a main course. Make one of the salsas from pages 17–20, Place the salsa on your dinner plates. Place the chiles on top of the salsa and serve at once.

Garnish: If you want a more complex taste and a greater visual flair, drizzle on one of the Zigzag Sauces (page 30) or some crema.

GOAT CHEESE, PINE NUT, *and* CORN FILLING

MAKES 2 CUPS

2 medium ears corn, kernels cut off

½ cup dried currants or dark raisins

6 ounces soft goat cheese

2 whole green onions, chopped

¼ cup chopped fresh cilantro,
leaves and tender stems

¼ cup pine nuts, toasted in a 325°F oven

2 cloves garlic, minced

1 teaspoon salt

½ teaspoon freshly ground black pepper

Combine all of the ingredients in a medium bowl and mix well. Proceed with stuffing and cooking the peppers according to your method of choice.

Seafood Variation: Make ½ recipe of the Goat Cheese Filling. Add ½ pound cooked medium shrimp or crabmeat or smoked salmon. Makes 2 cups. Proceed with stuffing and cooking the peppers.

Meat Variation: Make ½ recipe of the Goat Cheese Filling. Add ½ pound finely chopped or shredded cooked meat, such as Pulled Pork (page 146), smoked or grilled chicken, or cooked sausage. Makes 2 cups. Proceed with stuffing and cooking the peppers.

SQUASH BLOSSOM RELLENOS

SERVES 6 TO 8 AS AN APPETIZER OR FIRST COURSE

This recipe substitutes zucchini blossoms for the chile peppers. Zucchini blossoms can be found at farmers' markets during the summer.

12 zucchini blossoms

Your choice of filling (pages 59–60)

2 large eggs, well beaten

2 cups unbleached all-purpose flour

3 cups flavorless cooking oil

Gently stuff each blossom with ¼ cup of the filling. Just before cooking, dip the stuffed blossoms into the beaten eggs, then coat with the flour.

Pour the oil into a 12- to 14-inch frying pan. Turn the heat to high. When the oil becomes hot enough that the tip of a wooden spoon placed in the oil bubbles (375°F), gently add half the stuffed blossoms. Cook until golden on both sides, about 2 minutes. Drain on a wire rack, and repeat with the remaining stuffed blossoms. Serve at once.

Three staple foods of traditional Mexican cooking are corn, beans, and squash.

PLAY WITH

ENCHILADAS

*T*he Real Academia Española defines the term *enchilada* as used in Mexico as a rolled corn tortilla stuffed with meat and covered with a tomato and chile sauce. *Enchilada* is the past participle of *enchilar*, meaning literally "to season (or decorate) with chile."

Enchiladas are one of Mexico's most famous national dishes. When ordered at restaurants, they are assembled at the last moment. This means heating corn tortillas, laying a filling in each tortilla, and either folding the tortillas in half or rolling the tortillas into a cylinder. After a brief cooking to heat the interior, the enchiladas are topped with a sauce and grated or crumbled cheese.

We prefer to do all the assembly in advance, and then bake them in the oven until piping hot. This is a process that requires the more durable commercially made tortilla. Fresh homemade tortillas are more fragile and can only be used if assembling the enchiladas at the last moment.

Portions: For a main course, count on 2 enchiladas per person.

The Wrap: Use corn tortillas. To soften, warm them over a gas burner or on a gas grill, heating them only enough to become pliable. Or warm them in the microwave (see page 13). Or dip them into hot oil for about 10 seconds, until they become pliable. A nice flavor addition is sprinkling ½ teaspoon of ancho chile powder (or an American chile powder spice blend) into the hot oil just before adding the tortillas.

The Filling: Meat or seafood must be cooked first and works best cut into bite-size pieces. In this way, the enchiladas cook quickly and the texture of the tortillas is not compromised. Count on 4 ounces (or ½ cup chopped or sliced) cooked meat or seafood per enchilada. Choices include grilled chicken or pork, Pulled Pork (page 146), ground or link sausages cooked in advance, leftover meat from a pot roast or

One of the local traditions in the Central Bajio area is carving patterns into mesquite hardwood, and using herbal dyes to color tortillas for weddings and country fiestas.

stew, cooked shrimp or crabmeat, or grilled fish such as salmon, sea bass, or black cod.

Vegetarian: If making vegetarian enchiladas, choose one or more of the following: caramelized onions, sautéed mushrooms, matchstick-cut carrots, sliced Japanese eggplant cut into strips and grilled until soft and charred, charred bell peppers, and grilled or blanched asparagus. Avoid using high-moisture vegetables such as cabbages, spinach, and bean sprouts. The moisture in these vegetables can cause the enchiladas to become watery.

Cheese Enchiladas: Add the following to any meat, seafood, or vegetarian enchiladas, or use only cheese as the filling: Chihuahua, Monterey Jack, mild cheddar, pecorino, Emmenthaler, Gruyère, Muenster, crumbled queso fresco, or soft goat cheese.

Sauces: Replace any enchilada sauce with one of the following: Salsa Mexicana (page 17), Tomatillo Salsa (page 18), Mexican Chile Sauce (page 22), Ancho Chile Jam (page 23), Achiote Sauce (page 103), Mole Sauce (page 122), or Green Mole Sauce (page 125).

Garnish: Enhance the look, color, and texture of enchiladas by adding one or more chopped fresh herbs (parsley, cilantro, basil, or mint), crumbled queso fresco, crema, diced roasted bell peppers, chopped toasted pecans, toasted pine nuts, toasted pepitas, or one of the Zigzag Sauces on page 30.

Side Dishes: Enchiladas are usually served with Refried Beans (page 29) and Mexican Rice Pilaf (page 150). But why not think outside the box by choosing one of the following: an appetizer of Salmon and Scallop Ceviche (page 37), Chilled Avocado Soup (page 94), a side of Spicy Papaya Salad (page 76), and a dessert of Fallen Kahlúa Chocolate Cake (page 177).

MUSHROOM ENCHILADAS
with SALSA MEXICANA AND CREMA

SERVES 4

The Mexican sausage chorizo adds a wonderful richness to the mushroom filling. If you can't find raw chorizo, substitute another raw link sausage meat. Don't use the cured Spanish-style chorizo. The mushroom filling is delicious made with the more common cremini or button mushrooms, but it becomes a taste sensation if you substitute fresh porcini, enoki, and/or royal trumpet mushrooms.

8 ounces chorizo raw link sausage

8 ounces shiitake mushrooms

8 ounces cremini mushrooms

3 tablespoons olive oil, if needed

3 whole green onions

3 cloves garlic, minced

½ teaspoon salt

4 ounces Gruyère or mild cheddar cheese, coarsely grated

Salsa Mexicana (page 17)

8 (6-inch) corn tortillas

½ cup crema

½ cup queso fresco

Squeeze the sausage out of its casing. Place a 12-inch sauté pan over medium-low heat. When the pan becomes hot, add the sausage. Sauté the sausage, breaking it up into small pieces. When it loses its raw color, transfer the sausage meat to a cutting board, and chop it into small pieces.

Discard the shiitake mushroom stems and thinly slice all of the mushrooms. If there is no fat remaining in the sauté pan, add 3 tablespoons olive oil. Return the sauté pan to medium heat. When hot, add the mushrooms. Sauté until the mushrooms lose all their moisture and become densely textured, about 6 minutes. Meanwhile, chop the green onions and add to the sauté pan along with the sausage, garlic, and salt. Transfer to a bowl. You should have 4 cups of the mushroom filling. Stir in half of the grated cheese.

Prepare the salsa. Warm the tortillas as described on page 13.

Spread 1 cup of the salsa across the bottom of a 9 by 13-inch baking dish. Place ½ cup of the mushroom mixture in the center of a tortilla, and either roll into a cylinder or fold in half. Repeat with the remaining filling and tortillas and place side by side in the baking dish. Spoon on the remaining salsa. The recipe can be made up to this point 6 hours in advance and kept refrigerated.

To cook, preheat the oven to 350°F. Sprinkle the enchiladas with the remaining grated cheese. Bake until the sauce begins to bubble, about 30 minutes. Drizzle on the crema and crumbled queso fresco. Serve at once.

RED and GREEN CHICKEN ENCHILADAS

SERVES 4

Here the chicken filling is coated in a red sauce. Before baking, a tomatillo salsa and a spicy red sauce are spooned on the enchiladas to give the enchiladas two radically different colors. To speed preparation time, use a whole roasted chicken from the supermarket deli.

1 cup Mexican Chile Sauce (page 22)

1½ cups chopped vine-ripened tomatoes

½ teaspoon salt

½ cup chopped fresh cilantro, leaves and tender stems, divided in half

Meat from 1 whole roasted chicken

3 ears white corn

6 ounces Chihuahua or medium-sharp cheddar cheese, shredded

Tomatillo Salsa (page 18)

1 cup flavorless cooking oil

½ teaspoon ancho chile powder

8 (6-inch) corn tortillas

1 cup chopped red onion

½ cup crema or sour cream

Place the Mexican chile sauce in a bowl. Then add the chopped tomato, salt, and half of the cilantro. Cut the chicken into bite-size pieces or pull the meat into shreds. Cut the corn kernels off the cobs. In a bowl, place the chicken, corn, 1 cup of the Mexican chile-tomato sauce, and half of the cheese. Toss to evenly combine. Make the tomatillo salsa.

Place a 10-inch frying pan over medium-high heat and add the flavorless cooking oil. When the oil makes the edge of a tortilla bubble when dipped into the oil, sprinkle the chile powder over the oil. Dip each corn tortilla into the oil for 5 to 10 seconds, then drain on paper towels. Pat the top of the tortillas with paper towels to remove any extra oil.

Spread ½ cup of the Mexican chile-tomato sauce across the bottom of a 9 by 13-inch baking dish. Place ⅛ of the chicken-corn mixture in a tortilla and either roll into a cylinder or fold the tortilla in half. Repeat with the remaining chicken mixture and tortillas, and place the tortillas side by side in the baking dish. The recipe can be made up to this point 6 hours in advance and kept refrigerated.

Preheat the oven to 350°F. Pour the tomatillo salsa over half of the enchiladas, coating them evenly. Spoon the remaining Mexican chile-tomato sauce over the rest of the enchiladas. Sprinkle with the remaining grated cheese. Bake until the sauce begins to bubble, about 30 minutes. Sprinkle with the remaining cilantro and the red onion, and drizzle with the crema. Serve at once.

CHAPTER 5

SALAD SURPRISES

JICAMA SALAD

SERVES 8

Every market in Mexico has large displays of this brown-skinned round tuber. The crunchy white interior is cut into strips and sprinkled with ancho chile to be eaten as a snack, used as a garnish for cocktails, or as the main ingredient for salad. For more about jicama, see page 11. This salad is a lovely contrast of textures, colors, and flavors.

JICAMA SALAD DRESSING

¼ cup freshly squeezed lime juice

3 tablespoons extra-virgin olive oil

3 tablespoons honey

1 teaspoon ancho chile powder, or 1 tablespoon chipotle chiles in adobo sauce

½ teaspoon ground cumin

½ teaspoon salt

1 small garlic clove, minced

¼ cup chopped fresh cilantro, leaves and tender stems

⌒

1 pound jicama

1 red bell pepper

4 cups baby lettuce greens or arugula

2 cups pecan halves

To make the dressing, combine all of the ingredients in a small bowl. This can be done 12 hours in advance; keep refrigerated in a sealed container.

To make the salad, preheat the oven to 325°F. Use a paring knife to peel the jicama. Cut the jicama in half and then cut each half into very thin slices. Overlap the slices and cut into ¼-inch-thick shreds. You will need 4 cups.

Seed the red bell pepper and cut it into shreds. Put the greens in a large salad bowl. Toast the pecans on a baking sheet in the oven for 15 minutes, until they darken slightly and begin to smell. Let cool to room temperature. This recipe can be completed up to 24 hours in advance and refrigerated.

To assemble, add the jicama, red bell pepper, and nuts to the salad greens. Toss gently to combine. Give the dressing a stir and then pour over the salad. Toss all the ingredients again and serve.

Sticks of jicama and cucumber are commonly sold as snack food.

MEXICAN SLAW

SERVES 4

Derived from the Dutch words *cool sla*, meaning "cabbage salad," coleslaw is easy to overlook. But these days, chefs are combining shredded cabbage with flavorful combinations of oil, vinegar, and fresh herbs to provide a new image. We put a Mexican flavor twist on this by using chipotle chile in adobo sauce. The spicy, smoky flavor makes the slaw an ideal side dish to serve with barbecued meats or seafood, and with tacos.

½ head red or green cabbage
(or use a combination)

2 red bell peppers

½ cup pine nuts or pecans

1½ cups torn arugula

COLESLAW DRESSING

1 tablespoon minced fresh ginger

1 clove garlic, minced

2 small whole green onions, minced

¼ cup chopped fresh mint leaves

⅓ cup red or white wine vinegar

2 tablespoons light brown sugar

½ cup extra-virgin olive oil

1 tablespoon chipotle chile in adobo sauce

½ teaspoon salt

½ teaspoon freshly grated nutmeg

To make the salad, preheat the oven to 325°F. Cut off and discard the cabbage stem. Shred enough cabbage to make 6 cups. Discard the stems and seeds from the red peppers and then shred them. Spread the pine nuts on a baking sheet and toast in the oven until light golden, about 8 minutes. Set aside the arugula in the refrigerator.

To make the dressing, combine the ginger, garlic, green onions, mint, vinegar, brown sugar, olive oil, chipotle chile, salt, and nutmeg in an electric mini chopper or a blender. Chop or blend on high speed for 15 seconds. The recipe can be completed to this point 2 days before serving, with the components refrigerated in airtight containers.

To assemble, within 4 hours of serving, in a large bowl, combine the cabbage and bell pepper. Add the dressing and toss to combine well. Refrigerate if not serving right away. Just before serving, toss in the arugula and nuts.

AVOCADO SALAD *with* SEARED TUNA

SERVES 4 TO 6

This is one of the few entrée salads in the book. Make it the centerpiece of a Mexican dinner party. Assign tasks! Everyone contributes by bringing a dish. Start with Summer Rolls with Apples and Chipotle (page 39), then Quesadillas with Papaya and Brie (page 44), both served as "stand-up" appetizers. Wash these down with Blended Margaritas (page 192) and Cucumber Tea (page 187). Then adjourn to the dining table to enjoy the rich-tasting Sopa Azteca (page 91) served with a dry white wine. Now comes your contribution, Avocado Salad with Seared Tuna accompanied by warm dinner rolls. And for dessert, big bowls of Roasted Banana Ice Cream with Caramel Sauce (page 168). Note: You won't need all the salad dressing, but whatever remains will keep refrigerated for a week. Use it for other salad combinations, or as a sauce spooned over fish just removed from the barbecue or broiler.

1 pound sushi-grade tuna

2 tablespoons Mexican Dry Rub #1 (page 26)

2 tablespoons extra virgin olive oil

3 corn tortillas

1 cup flavorless cooking oil

GINGER-HERB SALAD DRESSING

¼ cup extra-virgin olive oil

¼ cup freshly squeezed lime juice

¼ cup mayonnaise

2 tablespoons honey

2 tablespoons Worcestershire sauce

2 tablespoons chopped fresh ginger

½ teaspoon ancho chile powder (optional)

¼ teaspoon salt

¼ cup parsley sprigs

¼ cup fresh mint leaves

◝

2 avocados

2 cups torn arugula, baby spinach, or baby field greens

There is a thriving organic and sustainable farming movement around San Miguel, spurred on by chefs who want the freshest ingredients, such as luscious avocados.

To make the salad, cut the tuna into logs, about 1 inch thick and 4 inches long. Rub all sides of the tuna with the dry rub. Then rub the olive oil on all sides of the tuna. Place a cast-iron skillet over high heat. After 5 minutes, add the tuna. Sear the tuna for 15 seconds on each side, 1 minute total cooking. Remove the tuna and chill in the refrigerator for 1 hour. Within 4 hours of serving time, thinly slice the tuna. Gently press plastic wrap across the tuna so that it is airtight, and refrigerate.

Cut the corn tortillas into ¼-inch strips. Place the cooking oil in a 10-inch frying pan over medium heat until a piece of tortilla floats immediately to the surface of the oil. Fry the tortilla strips in batches, removing them when they are brown. Drain on paper towels to remove any extra oil.

To make the dressing, combine all of the ingredients in a blender or food processor and blend to liquefy. The recipe can be completed up to this point 4 hours in advance with all food refrigerated except for the tortilla strips.

To assemble, cut the avocados in half, remove the pits, and scoop out the halves. Cut the avocado halves into thin slices. Place the arugula and avocado in a medium bowl. Pour in enough salad dressing to lightly coat all the ingredients, gently tossing to combine. You will need only ½ to ¾ cup of the dressing. The rest will keep refrigerated for 1 week. Transfer the salad to dinner or salad plates. Add the tortilla strips and the tuna. Serve at once.

SPICY PAPAYA SALAD

SERVES 4

The salad is great with 1 pound cooked chilled shrimp added. Or in place of the serrano chiles, use 1 to 2 tablespoons minced chipotle chiles in adobo sauce. It's the contrast between the floral tropical tastes of the papaya juxtaposed with the spicy heat from the chiles that makes this dish sing. A note on papaya: It should feel slightly firm to very firm. Perfectly ripe papaya will taste mushy.

½ cup pepitas (hulled pumpkin seeds)

4 slightly firm Hawaiian papayas, or 2 pounds Mexican papaya (you will need 8 cups cubed)

PAPAYA SALAD DRESSING

¼ cup chopped fresh ginger

2 serrano chiles, chopped, including the seeds, or Mexican hot sauce

¼ cup freshly squeezed lime juice

¼ cup extra-virgin olive oil

3 tablespoons light brown sugar

1 teaspoon ground cinnamon, preferably Mexican

½ teaspoon ground cumin

½ teaspoon salt

¼ cup chopped fresh mint leaves

To make the salad, place a sauté pan over medium heat, add the pumpkin seeds, and stir until light brown. Peel, seed, and cut the papaya into cubes (you will need 8 cups). We like the cubes to be large, at least 1 to 2 inches square.

To make the dressing, mince the ginger and serrano chiles in an electric mini chopper. Add the lime juice, olive oil, brown sugar, cinnamon, cumin, salt, and mint leaves. Pulse the mini chopper to liquefy. The recipe can be completed up to this point 12 hours before serving; keep the pumpkin seeds, papaya, and dressing refrigerated in airtight containers.

To assemble, place the papaya in a large bowl. Toss with the dressing. Transfer to salad plates, garnish with the toasted pumpkin seeds, and serve.

Fresh, sweet papaya in both red and orange colors makes a beautiful salad.

Fresh chiles, dried chiles, and fresh tomatillos abound in the produce markets.

YELLOW WATERMELON SALAD *with* EDIBLE FLOWERS
SERVES 4 TO 6

Edible flowers add a whimsical visual element to salads with their variations in color, shape, and texture. Dinner guests always express surprise, some asking suspiciously, "Are these safe to eat?!" Look for little plastic boxes of edible flowers in the produce section of supermarkets. These will be a mix of nasturtiums, chive blossoms, pansies, and violas. In this recipe, the combination of yellow watermelon, bright red Ancho Chile Jam, and edible flowers makes for a striking visual and taste celebration. For variation, replace the watermelon with honeydew melon.

3 pounds yellow watermelon

1 cup Ancho Chile Jam (page 23)

¼ cup crumbled queso fresco or crema

1 cup edible flower petals (optional)

Cut enough yellow watermelon into 2-inch cubes, rectangles, triangles, or other shapes to yield 8 cups. Knock away all seeds and refrigerate the watermelon. This can be done 12 hours before assembly. Stir the ancho chile jam. If it is very thick, thin with a little cold water so that it is thin enough to spread across a salad plate.

To serve, spread the ancho chili jam across salad plates. Place the yellow watermelon on top of the jam. To serve, garnish with a sprinkling of queso fresco and edible flowers, if using.

BEET AND ARUGULA SALAD *with* QUESO FRESCO

SERVES 4

Beet and arugula salads have become a wildly popular restaurant offering. We give this dish a Mexican twist by using a serrano-cinnamon dressing and sprinkling the salad with the Mexican cheese queso fresco. A nice variation is to use an equal amount of golden and red beets.

5 large red beets

½ cup slivered almonds

BEET SALAD DRESSING

½ cup extra-virgin olive oil

¼ cup crema

¼ cup rice vinegar

2 tablespoons freshly squeezed orange juice

2 tablespoons Worcestershire sauce

¼ cup chopped shallots

1 serrano chile, chopped, including the seeds

1 clove garlic, chopped

½ teaspoon ground cumin or cinnamon, preferably Mexican

½ teaspoon salt

4 cups arugula or mixed baby greens

½ cup crumbled queso fresco

To make the salad, preheat the oven to 400°F.

Scrub the beets. Place a 3-foot length of aluminum foil on a baking pan. Place the beets in the center of the foil. Draw the foil over the beets and seal to make a foil envelope. Roast in the oven for 1 hour. Remove from the oven and open the foil covering. Pierce the beets with the tines of a fork. If the tines do not sink easily into the beets, rewrap the beets with foil and roast for another 10 minutes. Remove from the oven. When the beets are still warm, using dry paper towels, rub off the skin. Cut the beets into 1-inch cubes.

Decrease the oven temperature to 325°F and toast the almonds on a baking sheet until golden, about 15 minutes.

To make the dressing, combine all of the ingredients in an electric mini chopper or blender. Blend at high speed for 15 seconds, then transfer to a small bowl. You can prepare the recipe up to this point 24 hours in advance, with all food kept refrigerated in airtight containers.

To assemble the salad, place the beets in a large bowl and add the arugula. Gently toss the ingredients, adding only enough salad dressing to coat the beets and arugula. You may not need to use all the salad dressing. Transfer the beet salad to serving plates. Sprinkle with the toasted almonds and queso fresco and serve.

CREAMY NOODLE SALAD *with* CUCUMBER AND PEPITAS

SERVES 6 TO 8

Make this pasta salad a starting point for your own creations. Choose your favorite pasta and vary the vegetables. Choose one or more of the following: cherry tomatoes, blanched asparagus, matchstick-cut jicama, shredded celery root or fennel, thinly sliced white button mushrooms, or enoki mushrooms whose compost ends are discarded and then the slender threads separated. Note: You will have extra peanut dressing. It will keep refrigerated for up to 2 weeks and is excellent spooned onto meat just removed from the grill.

8 ounces fusilli, penne, or your favorite pasta

4 Japanese cucumbers or 1 hothouse cucumber

½ cup chopped fresh cilantro, leaves and tender stems

½ cup pepitas (hulled pumpkin seeds), or ¼ cup white sesame seeds

PEANUT SALAD DRESSING

½ cup chunky peanut butter

1 cup freshly squeezed orange juice

¼ cup extra-virgin olive oil

¼ cup freshly squeezed lime juice

1 tablespoon chipotle chile in adobo sauce

2 cloves garlic, chopped

½ teaspoon salt

∽

1 orange

Cook the pasta according to the package directions. When tender but still firm, drain, rinse with cold water, and drain again.

Cut the cucumbers on a sharp diagonal into ¼-inch-wide slices. Overlap the slices and cut the cucumbers into matchstick pieces. Chop the cilantro. Place a small heavy frying pan over high heat. Add the pepitas and cook until they are lightly browned, 5 minutes, then tip out of the pan.

To make the dressing, combine all of the ingredients in a blender and liquefy. The recipe can be completed up to this point 24 hours prior to assembly, with the food kept refrigerated in airtight containers.

To assemble the salad, bring all the ingredients to room temperature, if necessary. In a large bowl, put the pasta, cucumbers, and cilantro. Gently toss. Pour in small amounts of the salad dressing and gently toss until evenly combined. (You will have salad dressing left over.) Transfer to serving plates. Using a Microplane, create a dusting of finely grated orange zest over the top of the salad. Sprinkle on the pepitas.

CAESAR SALAD *with* CHILE CROUTONS

SERVES 4

Caesar salad originated not in Italy but in Mexico! It was invented in the 1920s by an Italian chef and restaurant owner, Caesar Cardini, in the town of Tijuana. According to the family story (the family still operates the restaurant), one night Caesar ran out of salad dressing, so he made a quick concoction in a large wooden salad bowl of whole hearts of romaine, croutons, extra-virgin olive oil, lemon juice, and freshly grated Parmigiano-Reggiano. Originally the salad dressing was emulsified with a raw egg, but this recipe uses mayonnaise. And the anchovies are optional!

½ cup extra-virgin olive oil

3 cloves garlic, minced

1 teaspoon crushed red pepper

½ teaspoon salt

3 cups country-style white bread cut into ½-inch cubes

CAESAR SALAD DRESSING

2 cloves garlic, peeled

4 oil-packed anchovies (optional)

½ cup extra-virgin olive oil

¼ cup freshly squeezed lime or lemon juice

¼ cup Worcestershire sauce

3 tablespoons mayonnaise

½ teaspoon salt

4 small hearts of romaine, leaves separated

3 ears white sweet corn, kernels cut off cobs (only if available)

1 cup freshly grated Parmigiano-Reggiano cheese

Preheat the oven to 350°F.

Place the olive oil, garlic, crushed red pepper, and salt in a bowl. Add the bread cubes and toss immediately to evenly coat. Spread on a baking sheet and bake until light golden brown, about 20 minutes. Cool, then store in a resealable bag at room temperature or in the freezer.

To make the dressing, place all of the ingredients in a blender. Blend until smooth. This can be completed up to 8 hours before assembly and kept refrigerated in an airtight container.

To assemble the salad, position all the romaine leaves pointing in the same direction in a large serving bowl. Add the corn. Shake the salad dressing, pour over the leaves, and gently toss, adding only enough salad dressing to lightly coat the lettuce. Add the croutons and ½ cup of the cheese, and toss to evenly combine. Taste and adjust the seasonings, adding salt and freshly ground black pepper to taste. Arrange on serving plates. Sprinkle with the remaining ½ cup cheese. Serve at once.

BBQ CAESAR SALAD

This salad will amaze your dinner guests. I thought it was a crazy idea initially. How could one possibly grill romaine without it being reduced to a soggy mess? Actually, what you need is a very hot grill. The quick cooking allows the lettuce to develop a nice char without any wilting. But if one errs on the side of caution and plays it safe by lowering the heat, the romaine will never char—it will wilt.

4 small whole hearts of romaine
(do not separate the leaves)

Extra-virgin olive oil, for brushing

Caesar Salad Dressing, for serving

Chile Croutons, for serving

Prepare a hot fire in a gas or charcoal grill. If the hearts of romaine are large, then cut them in half lengthwise using a serrated knife. Place the romaine in a large bowl. Toss with enough olive oil to lightly coat the outside leaves. Place the romaine on the hot grill, and lightly char on one side. Turn the romaine over and char on the opposite side (about 15 seconds per side).

Place the grilled romaine on serving plates. Spoon the Caesar salad dressing over the romaine. Sprinkle with the croutons. Serve at once.

The country-style barbeque warms
up with a mesquite wood fire.

MEXICAN CHOPPED CAESAR SALAD
with CHILE-GARLIC TORTILLAS

SERVES 4

We tasted this Caesar salad recently while staying at a resort near Cabo San Lucas in Baja California. Unlike a traditional Caesar salad, which is served whole leaf, here the romaine is chopped and tossed with chile-garlic tortilla strips. And if you are part of the anti-anchovy camp, substitute Chinese oyster sauce. Its rich taste makes a great flavor variation.

1 cup flavorless cooking oil

2 cloves garlic, minced

4 (6-inch) corn tortillas, cut into ¼-inch-wide strips (use blue or red corn tortillas if available)

1 teaspoon crushed red pepper or ancho chile powder

½ teaspoon salt

4 hearts of romaine, leaves separated

3 ears white sweet corn (only if available), shucked

Extra-virgin olive oil, for brushing

Caesar Salad Dressing, for serving (page 80)

1 cup freshly grated Parmigiano-Reggiano cheese

1 lemon or lime

Prepare a medium fire in a gas or charcoal grill.

Place the cooking oil and garlic in a 10-inch frying pan. Heat the oil until a strip of tortilla added to it bubbles around the edges. Cook the tortilla strips in small batches until dark golden, about 2 minutes. Then remove the strips with a slotted spoon and transfer to a layer of paper towels to drain. When all the tortillas are fried, sprinkle them with crushed red pepper and salt, then toss gently.

Cut the romaine lettuce into shreds. Rub the corn with extra-virgin olive oil, then lightly char on the grill. When cool enough to handle, cut off the kernels. The recipe can be completed up to this point 8 hours ahead, with the food kept refrigerated (except for the tortilla strips).

In a large bowl, combine the romaine lettuce and corn. Shake the salad dressing, pour the dressing over the leaves, and gently toss, adding only enough salad dressing to lightly coat the lettuce. Add the crisp tortilla strips and ½ cup of the grated cheese, and gently toss with the romaine. Place on serving plates. Sprinkle with the lime zest and the remaining ½ cup cheese. Using a microplane, grate the lemon or lime over the top of the salad. Serve at once.

TOMATO SALAD *with* QUESO FRESCO

SERVES 4

Make this salad only when tomatoes are at the height of their season. Use a variety of heirloom tomatoes, with their varying acidity and colors.

TOMATO SALAD DRESSING

5 tablespoons extra-virgin olive oil

3 tablespoons freshly squeezed lime juice

1 chipotle chile in adobo sauce

¼ cup loosely packed cilantro sprigs

1 clove garlic, peeled

½ teaspoon salt

∽

8 ounces queso fresco, goat cheese, or fresh mozzarella

¼ cup pepitas (hulled pumpkin seeds)

6 medium vine-ripened tomatoes, various colors

To make the dressing, combine all of the ingredients in an electric mini chopper or a blender. Blend on high speed for 15 seconds.

To make the salad, cut the queso fresco into 8 pieces. In a small frying pan, toast the pepitas over high heat until they begin to make a popping noise, 1 to 2 minutes. The recipe can be prepared up to this point 24 hours in advance, with the food refrigerated in airtight containers.

To assemble the salad, cut off and discard the tomato stems. Cut the tomatoes into various sizes and shapes. Arrange the tomatoes and cheese on serving plates. Stir the salad dressing and pour it around the edges of the tomatoes. Sprinkle with the pepitas and serve at room temperature.

CHAPTER 6

COMPLEX-TASTING SOUPS

YELLOW GAZPACHO *with* GINGER

SERVES 4 AS A FIRST COURSE

Every summer during the height of the tomato season, Teri makes this soup from perfectly ripe yellow tomatoes bought at our local farmers' market. Taking only about 30 minutes to prepare, the soup has a striking yellow color speckled with green flecks of cilantro. The soup is also very good made with red tomatoes. But if you do that, omit the vinegar, since red tomatoes have enough acid. For variation, just before serving, stir in chilled cooked shrimp or fresh lump crabmeat.

3 large vine-ripened yellow tomatoes, about 1½ pounds

½ yellow bell pepper

2 green onions, white part only

¼ bunch cilantro, leaves and tender stems, about 1 cup loosely packed

½ jalapeño or serrano chile, including the seeds

3 cloves garlic, minced

1 tablespoon minced fresh ginger

¼ cup extra-virgin olive oil

1 teaspoon salt

¼ cup red or white wine vinegar, or as needed

Cut the tomatoes in half through the circumference (not through the stem). Place a sieve into a bowl. Over the sieve, gently shake out the tomato seeds. Reserve the tomato juice. Cut away the stem area, and cut the tomatoes into large cubes. Chop the bell pepper. Coarsely chop the green onions. Cut off and discard the large cilantro stems. Set aside a few sprigs of cilantro for garnish. Chop the chile.

Place the tomatoes, the tomato juice, the bell pepper, garlic, and ginger in a blender. Blend until liquefied. Add the green onions, cilantro, chile, olive oil, and salt. Pulse a few times. Taste the soup. Add the vinegar as desired, depending on how tart you want the soup. Makes approximately 4 cups. Refrigerate for 30 minutes before serving. The soup can be prepared up to 24 hours ahead and refrigerated in an airtight container.

To serve, first taste the soup again and adjust as needed for salt, spice, and vinegar. Serve in chilled bowls garnished with the cilantro sprigs.

SERRANO GAZPACHO SERVED *in* SHOT GLASSES

SERVES 4 AS A FIRST COURSE OR 8 AS AN APPETIZER

Successful appetizers have a flavor punch. The tiny tastes, or in this case the little sips, are a taste triumph only if packed with seasonings. This dish has so many levels of flavor that your guests will still be wondering about possible ingredients long after consuming the gazpacho. We serve this in shot glasses, tequila shooters, sake cups, martini glasses, or little Japanese teacups. For a nice variation, after the soup has been chilled, stir in a diced avocado.

6 cups quartered vine-ripened tomatoes

2 tablespoons Worcestershire sauce

2 cloves garlic, chopped

1 to 2 serrano chiles, chopped, including the seeds

¼ cup fresh cilantro, leaves and tender stems

½ teaspoon salt

1 lime (optional)

½ cup crumbled queso fresco or crema

Finely chop by hand 2 cups of the quartered tomatoes.

In a blender, place the remaining 4 cups quartered tomatoes, the Worcestershire, garlic, chiles, cilantro, and salt. Blend until smooth, and then transfer to a bowl. Stir in the chopped tomatoes. Refrigerate for 30 minutes before serving. The soup can be completed up to this point 2 days ahead and kept refrigerated in an airtight container.

To serve, taste and adjust the seasonings, especially for spice, salt, and lime, if using. Transfer to shot glasses or small soup bowls. Garnish with the crumbled queso fresco and serve.

SOPA AZTECA (*Tortilla Soup*)
SERVES 4

This is one of Mexico's most famous soups, and there are many variations. The dried chiles can be omitted. Or float a whole chipotle chile in adobo sauce in the center of each bowl of soup. Or stir shrimp (peeled and butterflied) into the soup for a few minutes of gentle simmering. At the end of this recipe, there are three suggestions for serving this soup: as an appetizer, as a first course, and as a main course with roasted or grilled chicken added.

3 (6-inch) corn tortillas

1 cup flavorless cooking oil

5 large vine-ripened tomatoes, about 3 pounds

3 tablespoons sugar

2 guajillo chiles

2 cups low-sodium chicken broth

2 small shallots, papery skin removed

4 cloves garlic, peeled

1 teaspoon salt

½ teaspoon dried oregano, or 2 teaspoons chopped fresh oregano, preferably Mexican

2 ripe avocados

¼ cup chopped fresh cilantro, leaves and tender stems

¼ cup crema

Lime wedges, for garnish

Cut the tortillas in half, then into ¼-inch-wide strips. Heat the cooking oil in a large frying pan until a piece of tortilla dipped into the oil bubbles. Add the tortilla strips and cook in batches until dark golden, about 1 minute. Drain on paper towels.

Prepare a hot fire in a gas or charcoal grill. Cut the tops and bottoms off the tomatoes. Cut the tomatoes in half horizontally and sprinkle both sides with the sugar. Place over the fire, and cook until charred on both sides, about 5 minutes per side. Discard the skins, and transfer the tomatoes to a blender.

Using scissors, cut the stems off the chiles. Shake out all interior seeds. In a small saucepan, bring the chicken broth to a boil. Then turn off the heat, add the chiles, and place a small bowl on top of the chiles to submerge them. Let soak for 30 minutes, then transfer the chiles and broth to the blender holding the tomatoes.

Cut the shallots in half. Place a small, heavy frying pan over medium-high heat. When hot, add the garlic cloves and shallots. Cook on both sides until lightly browned, about 2 minutes. Transfer the garlic and shallots to the blender. Add the salt and oregano. Blend on high speed for 30 seconds. Transfer the tomato soup to a large saucepan. The recipe can be completed up to this point 24 hours in advance, with the soup kept refrigerated in an airtight container.

When ready to serve, pit, peel, and slice the avocados.

continued on next page

Most houses in San Miguel have an outdoor living area, called an outdoor sala, where a leisurely lunch can be enjoyed in the shade.

To serve as an appetizer: Serve the tomato soup chilled in shooter glasses, garnished with the cilantro, crema, and lime wedges (omit the tortillas and avocado).

To serve as a first course: Bring the soup to a low simmer. Taste and adjust the seasonings. Ladle into soup bowls and garnish with the sliced avocado, tortilla strips, cilantro, and crema. Serve accompanied by lime wedges.

To serve as a main course: Bring the soup to a low simmer. Slice the meat from 1 roasted deli chicken into bite-size pieces. Place the chicken in the bottom of each bowl; ladle in the hot tomato soup. Garnish with the sliced avocado, crema, and lime wedges.

COCONUT-ANCHO SOUP *with* MUSHROOMS

SERVES 4 AS A FIRST COURSE

Coconut is a common ingredient along the southern coast of Mexico. Here dried chiles are simmered in the coconut broth, thus infusing the soup with flavor and tinting it a slight reddish color. The soup is also good served chilled in shooter glasses as an appetizer.

2 ancho chiles

4 cups unsweetened coconut milk (see page 10)

2 cups low-sodium chicken broth

½ serrano chile, chopped, including the seeds

2 cloves garlic, chopped

2 tablespoons chopped fresh ginger

1 (1-inch) cinnamon stick, preferably Mexican

2 teaspoons finely grated lime zest

1 teaspoon salt

3 ears sweet white corn, shucked

Salt and freshly ground black pepper

2 tablespoons extra-virgin olive oil, plus more for rubbing the corn

4 ounces mushrooms, such as shiitake or cremini

¼ cup shredded fresh mint leaves

8 lime wedges

Stem and seed the ancho chiles. Cut them into 6 pieces. In a 3-quart saucepan over medium heat, combine the ancho chiles, coconut milk, broth, serrano chile, garlic, ginger, cinnamon, lime zest, and salt. Bring to a simmer (but do not let the soup boil). Then turn off the heat and let it sit for 1 hour. Discard the cinnamon stick.

Pour the soup into a blender. Pulse on high speed for 30 seconds. Rub the corn with salt and pepper, then rub with a little olive oil. Roast the corn until lightly browned in a heavy frying pan over high heat (or grill it on a gas or charcoal grill). When cool enough to handle, cut the kernels off the cobs and stir them into the soup.

Cut the mushrooms into thin slices or into quarters. In a 2½-quart saucepan over medium heat, heat the 2 tablespoons olive oil. Add the mushrooms and sauté until they soften, about 3 minutes. Add the mushrooms to the corn-coconut broth. The soup can be completed up to this point 24 hours ahead, with the soup kept refrigerated in an airtight container.

To serve, bring the soup to a simmer over low heat. Ladle into Asian teacups or soup bowls. Garnish with the mint leaves and lime wedges.

CHILLED AVOCADO SOUP *with* ANCHO CHILE JAM

SERVES 6 AS A FIRST COURSE

Hugh first tasted this soup as a teenager spending the summer in Cuernavaca. Served iced in a tropical garden setting including giant macaws, the evening made an indelible impression. This very tasty and easy recipe can be made a day in advance and refrigerated. It maintains its vibrant green color. Serve it as a first course, or as an appetizer in sake cups or shot glasses, or pour the soup into martini glasses ringed with large chilled cooked shrimp. Another nice variation is to float an iceberg lettuce cup in the center of each bowl of avocado soup, and fill the lettuce cup with fresh cooked crabmeat or bay shrimp. Or, sprinkle a crumbled goat cheese or farmer's cheese over the top of the soup, or swirl in some crema. Of course, for this dish everything depends on choosing an avocado that is at a perfect ripeness. Look for buttery Hass avocados grown in Southern California or Mexico.

1 perfectly ripe avocado

2 to 4 tablespoons chopped fresh cilantro, leaves and tender stems

2 tablespoons chopped fresh ginger

½ serrano chile, finely minced, including the seeds

3 cups low-sodium chicken broth, plus more if needed

2 to 4 tablespoons freshly squeezed lime juice

½ teaspoon salt

4 to 8 squares iceberg lettuce, each 2 by 2 inches

Ancho Chile Jam, for serving (page 23)

Crema, for garnish

Cut the avocado in half, discard the pit, and scoop out the flesh. Transfer the avocado to a blender. Add the cilantro, ginger, serrano chile, broth, lime juice, and salt. Blend until liquefied. If the soup is too thick, thin it by adding more chicken broth.

Taste and adjust the flavors of chile, lime juice, and salt. Transfer to a bowl and press plastic wrap directly across the surface of the soup. Refrigerate for 30 minutes before serving. The soup can be prepared 24 hours ahead and kept refrigerated in an airtight container.

To serve, taste again and adjust the soup for chile, lime juice, and salt. Transfer the soup to chilled soup bowls, martini glasses, or shot glasses. If serving this in soup bowls, add the iceberg lettuce squares, and place a small spoonful of ancho chile jam in each iceberg lettuce square. If serving the soup in cups too small to hold the iceberg lettuce squares, add a little spoonful of the jam to the center of the soup. Drizzle a little crema over the top and serve at once.

This is a mango version of the avocado soup. Replace the avocado with 4 cups mango flesh. Place in blender with the remaining ingredients and puree.

WATERMELON SOUP

SERVES 4 AS A FIRST COURSE

We first enjoyed this soup many years ago at Juan Carlos Escalante's beautiful San Miguel restaurant, Nirvana. The soup made a lasting impression on us, and we have made many variations. This is the latest one! Buy seedless watermelon at the peak of the summer crop, when it has the brightest color. This is good hot or chilled, though we prefer it chilled. We've tried using red watermelon for the soup and yellow watermelon for the diced garnish. The two-color arrangement looks odd, however, so be consistent and use just one color of watermelon.

4 pounds watermelon

¼ cup freshly squeezed lime juice

2 tablespoons minced fresh ginger

½ serrano chile, chopped, including the seeds

1 tablespoon Worcestershire sauce

1 teaspoon salt

½ cup crema

¼ cup fresh mint leaves, shredded or chopped

Prepare 5 cups of watermelon cut into approximately 1-inch cubes. Remove the seeds. Prepare 2 cups of watermelon cut into ¼- to ½-inch dice. Remove the seeds. Set the diced watermelon aside.

Place the 5 cups cubed watermelon in a blender. Add the lime juice, ginger, chile, Worcestershire, and salt. Blend into a liquid. Place a medium-mesh sieve over a saucepan, and strain the soup through the sieve in order to remove any lingering seeds.

Bring the soup to a simmer over low heat and simmer for 10 minutes. The soup can be prepared up to this point 24 hours in advance and kept refrigerated in an airtight container. Makes 4 to 6 cups.

If serving the soup hot: Reheat in a saucepan over low heat, if necessary. Stir in the reserved diced watermelon. Taste the soup, adjusting for the salt and lime juice. Pour into soup bowls and garnish with the crema and mint.

If serving chilled: Stir in the reserved diced watermelon. Spoon the chilled soup into martini or shot glasses. Garnish with the crema and mint.

CILANTRO SOUP
with PRAWNS

SERVES 4 AS A MAIN COURSE

This recipe was inspired by Chef Robert Del Grande's famous cilantro and mussel soup that he served for many years at his Houston restaurant, Café Annie. We serve the soup on a hot summer night as the main course accompanied by Yellow Watermelon Salad (page 77), Mexican Spicy Smoked Baby Back Riblets (page 45), and Coconut Ice Cream (page 169).

1½ pounds raw large shrimp, shell on

2 tablespoons extra-virgin olive oil

5 cloves garlic, chopped

5 cups low-sodium chicken broth

2 bunches cilantro, including all the stems (8 cups loosely packed)

2 cups packed spinach

2 whole green onions, chopped

2 tablespoons chopped fresh ginger

1 serrano chile, chopped, including the seeds

1 teaspoon salt

2 cups heavy cream

Freshly ground black pepper

Olive oil

2 teaspoons cornstarch

Ancho Chile Jam, for garnish (page 23)

Peel the shrimp, saving the shells. Split the shrimp in half lengthwise. Rinse away any black vein, then set aside. In a medium saucepan over medium heat, place the olive oil, garlic, and shrimp shells. Cook for a few minutes, until the shells turn pink. Add the broth, bring to a simmer, cover, and cook over low heat for 15 minutes. Transfer to a blender. Blend on high speed for 15 seconds, then pour the liquid through a mesh sieve. Reserve the liquid and discard all solids.

Put the broth, cilantro, spinach, green onions, ginger, chile, and salt into the blender. Blend to liquefy. If you have a small blender, you may need to do this in batches. Transfer to a bowl. Stir in the cream. You will have 8 cups of soup. Taste and adjust the seasonings. The soup can be prepared up to this point 24 hours ahead and kept refrigerated in an airtight container.

To serve, prepare a medium fire in a gas or charcoal grill. Season the shrimp with salt, pepper, and olive oil. Grill the shrimp for about 2 minutes on each side, or until pink.

Combine the cornstarch with 2 teaspoons water. Bring the soup to a simmer. If you want a thicker soup, stir the cornstarch mixture into the soup. Pour the soup into shallow soup bowls. Add the shrimp and garnish with spoonfuls of ancho chile jam. Serve hot.

CHAPTER 7

SEAFOOD

Inspired by Mexico's Coast

BBQ SALMON *with* CHILE, TOMATOES, AND CUCUMBERS

SERVES 4

In this dish, the salmon is skinned, marinated on both sides, and then cooked on a bed of sliced oranges. The oranges will not burn away during cooking and will infuse the underside of the salmon with additional flavor. In fact, the charred orange slices are delicious. We serve the salmon on the charred orange slices and encourage our friends to taste the charred orange—it tastes great! As an excellent variation, stir a diced ripe avocado into the Spicy Tomato–Cucumber Salsa. In terms of the type of cucumber, use something with minimal seeds, like hothouse cucumbers, Middle Eastern cucumbers, or Japanese cucumbers.

SPICY TOMATO-CUCUMBER SALSA

1 cup finely chopped vine-ripened tomatoes

1 cup chopped seeded cucumber, not peeled

¼ cup freshly squeezed lime juice

¼ cup lightly packed light brown sugar

¼ cup chopped fresh cilantro, leaves and tender stems

¼ cup chopped green onion, green and white parts

2 tablespoons Worcestershire sauce

2 cloves garlic, minced

1 serrano chile, minced, including the seeds

½ teaspoon salt

4 (6-ounce) fresh salmon fillets, skin and pinbones removed

¼ cup thin soy sauce

¼ cup olive oil

3 cloves garlic, minced

1 teaspoon ground cinnamon or cumin

2 oranges

Rooms in most traditional homes are arranged around a patio with a fountain at its center.

To make the salsa, remove the tomato stems, but do not seed or peel the tomatoes. Finely chop the tomatoes. Combine the tomatoes, cucumber, lime juice, brown sugar, cilantro, green onion, Worcestershire, garlic, serrano chile, and salt in a medium bowl. The salsa can be prepared up to 24 hours ahead and kept refrigerated in an airtight container.

To prepare the fish, 2 hours prior to cooking, rub the salmon on both sides with the soy sauce, olive oil, garlic, and cinnamon. Remove the salsa from the fridge, if necessary, so it will come to room temperature. Cut the oranges into 8 round slices, each ¼ inch thick.

Prepare a medium-hot fire in a charcoal or gas grill. Place the orange slices in pairs, edge to edge over the direct heat. Place 1 piece of salmon on top of each pair of orange slices. Cover the grill. Cook for 10 minutes, never removing the cover. Then remove the cover and check the fish. If it does not begin to flake when prodded with a knife, cover the grill and cook for another 2 minutes.

Transfer the oranges with the salmon on top to serving plates. Using a slotted spoon, spoon the salsa over the fish and serve at once.

SCALLOPS *with* HERB BUTTER AND TOMATILLO SALSA

SERVES 4

Because this dish needs about 10 minutes of last-minute attention, we make this for small gatherings and as the only Mexican-inspired dish in the dinner. In this way, Mexico's unique flavors are highlighted. But if you wish, accompany the scallops with one of the rice dishes, such as Coconut or Saffron Rice Pilaf (page 151).

2 pounds fresh sea scallops

1 ripe avocado

Tomatillo Salsa (page 18)

1 cup salted butter, at room temperature

4 cloves garlic, minced

2 tablespoons minced fresh ginger

¼ cup packed fresh cilantro, leaves and tender stems, or mint leaves, chopped

Finely grated zest of 2 limes

½ teaspoon salt

4 ounces queso fresco or goat cheese, crumbled

2 limes, cut into wedges

Pull off and discard the little extra muscle that is attached to one side of each sea scallop. Set aside. Pit, peel, and dice the avocado, and then stir it into the tomatillo salsa.

Cut the butter into small pieces. In a small saucepan, combine the butter, garlic, ginger, cilantro, lime zest, and salt. Bring to a simmer. The recipe can be completed up to this point 24 hours in advance and stored by refrigerating the butter sauce, scallops, and salsa.

When ready to serve, prepare a medium-hot fire in a gas or charcoal grill. Bring the butter sauce to a simmer. Toss the scallops in the butter. Spoon the tomatillo salsa across the bottom of warm serving plates.

Add the scallops to the grill grate in a single layer. Cook the scallops on both sides until the scallops begin to feel firm when pressed with a finger, about 5 minutes for large scallops. Use an offset spatula or barbecue tongs to turn the scallops.

Place the scallops on top of the tomatillo salsa. Garnish with the crumbled queso fresco and lime wedges. Serve at once.

SEAFOOD *with* ACHIOTE SAUCE

SERVES 4

The recipe will take about 60 minutes to prepare, but almost everything can be made well in advance of cooking. It's an ideal dish for inviting a cooking friend for dinner. That way you'll have help stirring in the seafood and plating the dish. Serve this with one of the rice dishes from Chapter 8. With a couple of the dinner guests bringing appetizers and a dessert, the dinner takes on more of a collective spirit, and everyone has more fun.

1 pound fresh sea or bay scallops

½ pound fresh salmon fillet, skin and pinbones removed

½ pound large raw shrimp

1 ancho chile, stem and seeds removed

2 cups low-sodium chicken broth

1 cup freshly squeezed orange juice

2 ounces achiote paste

2 tablespoons light brown sugar

1 tablespoon chopped fresh oregano, preferably Mexican

½ teaspoon salt

2 tablespoons vegetable or olive oil

½ medium white onion, chopped

4 cloves garlic, chopped

1 (1½-inch) cinnamon stick, preferably Mexican

1 ripe avocado

Crumbled queso fresco or crema, for garnish

If using sea scallops, remove the muscle attached to each scallop and discard. Thinly slice the sea scallops. Cut the salmon into ½-inch-thick strips, then cut the strips into 1½-inch lengths. Peel and devein the shrimp.

Using scissors, cut open the ancho chile and discard all the seeds and stem. Bring the chicken broth to a boil. Place the ancho chile in a small bowl and cover with the boiling chicken broth. After 30 minutes, in a blender, place the ancho chile, all of the chicken broth, orange juice, achiote paste, brown sugar, oregano, and salt. Puree until liquefied.

Place a heavy 3-quart saucepan over medium heat. Add the oil, onion, and garlic. Cook until the onion and garlic brown, about 10 minutes. Add the orange juice mixture, plus the cinnamon stick. Simmer for about 20 minutes or until the sauce becomes thick enough to coat a spoon. Discard the cinnamon stick. The sauce can be made up to 3 days ahead and kept refrigerated in an airtight container.

When ready to serve, bring the sauce to a simmer in a large saucepan over low heat, if necessary. Stir in the seafood and simmer until cooked, about 3 minutes. Pit, peel, and slice the avocado. Transfer the seafood to warm dinner plates. Garnish with the queso fresco and slices of avocado and serve at once.

BBQ SHRIMP *with* SPICY WATERMELON SAUCE

SERVES 4

This brilliantly red sauce has a lingering taste and is a striking visual contrast to the barbecued shrimp. The sauce is also great served with grilled halibut or sea bass. Although the shrimp are grilled in this recipe, you can also sauté the shrimp in a 14-inch frying pan or roast them in a 450°F oven.

SPICY WATERMELON SAUCE

4 cups cubed seedless red watermelon, plus 2 cups chopped watermelon

1 cup dry red wine, such as Zinfandel or Cabernet Sauvignon

1 tablespoon hot sauce of your choice

½ teaspoon salt

2 tablespoons minced fresh ginger

∽

2 pounds large raw shrimp

¼ cup olive oil

2 tablespoons finely minced fresh ginger

1 teaspoon cornstarch

½ cup crumbled queso fresco

3 tablespoons slivered fresh mint leaves

1 lime, cut into 8 wedges

To prepare the sauce, place 4 cups cubed watermelon, the wine, hot sauce, salt, and ginger in a blender. Blend to liquefy. Transfer to a 12-inch sauté pan and boil over medium-high heat for about 6 minutes until reduced to 2 cups. Taste and adjust the seasonings, if needed. The sauce can be prepared up to 24 hours ahead and kept refrigerated in an airtight container.

Peel the shrimp and cut deeply along the top ridge. Rinse away the black vein, if present. In a small bowl, combine the olive oil and ginger. Rub the shrimp with the oil-ginger mixture. Refrigerate the shrimp up to 4 hours before cooking.

Prepare a medium-hot fire in a gas or charcoal grill. Grill the shrimp, turning them several times, until they turn white in the center (cut into a shrimp to check), about 3 minutes total. Bring the watermelon sauce to a simmer, if necessary. Dissolve the cornstarch in 1 teaspoon cold water. Stir this into the sauce. Add the remaining 2 cups chopped watermelon. Spoon the watermelon sauce onto warm serving plates. Transfer the shrimp to the center of the watermelon sauce. Sprinkle with the queso fresco and mint, and serve accompanied by lime wedges.

SHRIMP *with* MEXICAN PESTO

SERVES 4

What's Mexican about this recipe? It's the use of serrano chiles and cilantro in the pesto and the rub of cumin, black pepper, and lime zest on the shrimp. The dish will have even more Mexican flavor if you make wraps with warm tortillas, avocado slices, and salsa. If you are cooking for a larger group, place the shrimp in a single layer on a baking sheet, and roast the shrimp in a preheated 450°F oven until they turn white in the center when cut into (not opaque), about 5 minutes.

MEXICAN PESTO

1 clove garlic, peeled

2 tablespoons thinly sliced fresh ginger

1 serrano chile, cut into small pieces, including the seeds

½ cup packed fresh cilantro, leaves and tender stems

½ cup packed fresh basil leaves

½ cup packed fresh mint leaves

2 tablespoons fresh oregano leaves, preferably Mexican

¼ cup toasted walnuts, pecans, or pine nuts

¼ cup grated Italian Parmigiano-Reggiano cheese

⅓ cup extra-virgin olive oil

1 tablespoon light brown sugar

½ teaspoon salt

Freshly squeezed juice of 1 lime

ᔐ

1½ pounds raw large shrimp

½ teaspoon ground cumin

1 teaspoon freshly ground black pepper

½ teaspoon salt

1 tablespoon finely grated lime zest

3 tablespoons extra-virgin olive oil

ᔐ

1 red bell pepper, stemmed, seeded, and chopped

Palm trees of many varieties are highly prized for patios.

To make the pesto sauce, mince the garlic and ginger in a food processor. Add the serrano chile and mince again. Add the cilantro, basil, mint, and oregano and mince again. Add the walnuts and cheese, then mince again briefly. Add the olive oil, brown sugar, salt, and lime juice. Mince until it forms a paste, adding more olive oil if necessary. Transfer to a bowl and press plastic wrap directly across the surface of the pesto. The pesto can be prepared up to 24 hours ahead and kept refrigerated in an airtight container.

Peel the shrimp and cut deeply along the top ridge. Rinse away the black vein, if present. Rub the shrimp with the cumin, pepper, salt, lime zest, and olive oil, adding these one at a time and rubbing each evenly all over the shrimp. Set aside in the refrigerator.

To finish, make sure the pesto is at room temperature. Place a 12- or 14-inch sauté pan over high heat. When it becomes very hot, add the shrimp. Stir and toss until the shrimp turn white in the center (cut into a shrimp to check), about 3 minutes.

Stir the pesto and spread the center of each serving plate with a thick smear. Mound the shrimp on top of the pesto. Garnish with the chopped red bell pepper and serve at once.

ROAST FISH *with* PINEAPPLE-COCONUT GLAZE

SERVES 4

This is an easy recipe yielding a fantastic result. The fish is just rubbed with a simple mix of seasonings and then roasted in the oven with very little supervision. And the ingredients for the glaze can be combined hours ahead in a saucepan, and then brought to a low boil just before being spooned over the cooked fish.

2 pounds firm fresh fish fillets such as sea bass, black cod, or salmon cut into 4 pieces

1 teaspoon pure Mexican chile powder, such as ancho chile powder

1 teaspoon salt

¼ cup extra-virgin olive oil

PINEAPPLE-COCONUT GLAZE

1 red bell pepper, stemmed, seeded, and diced

1 cup chopped fresh pineapple

1 cup unsweetened coconut milk (see page 10)

½ cup low-sodium chicken broth

2 teaspoons finely grated lime zest

1 teaspoon salt

¼ cup chopped fresh mint leaves

3 tablespoons flavorless cooking oil

4 cloves garlic, minced

2 tablespoons minced fresh ginger

1 serrano chile, minced, including the seeds

2 limes, cut into wedges

Rub the fish on both sides with the chile, salt, and olive oil.

To make the glaze, in a bowl, combine the red bell pepper, pineapple, coconut milk, chicken broth, lime zest, salt, and mint. In a large saucepan over medium heat, combine the cooking oil, garlic, ginger, and chile. Sauté until the garlic begins to brown, about 15 seconds. Add the coconut-pineapple mixture. Bring to a low boil, then remove from the heat. The glaze can be prepared up to 8 hours before serving and kept refrigerated in an airtight container.

Preheat the oven to 325°F. Line a baking sheet with aluminum foil and spray the foil with nonstick cooking spray.

Place the fish on the prepared baking sheet. Roast in the oven until the fish just begins to flake, about 12 minutes. Meanwhile, in a small saucepan bring the coconut sauce to a simmer.

Transfer the fish to serving plates. Spoon the sauce over the fish. Serve accompanied with lime wedges.

SHRIMP *with* CHILE-TANGERINE SAUCE

SERVES 4

If I could choose one favorite recipe in this book, this recipe would be near or at the top. But triumph depends on certain key elements. The guajillo chiles must be pliable and not old and wrinkled. Use only tangerines, not oranges, and freshly squeeze the juice within 8 hours of use. Pay attention to the shrimp: The shrimp should arrive at the fishmonger from their ocean home and not be the tasteless black tiger prawns that are farm-raised in Asia. Now go in the kitchen and create some magic.

1½ pounds raw large shrimp

2 tablespoons flavorless cooking oil

2 large cloves garlic, minced

2 tablespoons minced fresh ginger

2 guajillo chiles

1 cup freshly squeezed tangerine juice

¼ cup white wine vinegar

¼ cup lightly packed light brown sugar

½ teaspoon salt

2 tangerines

2 teaspoons cornstarch

1 whole nutmeg

¼ cup chopped fresh cilantro, leaves and tender stems

Peel the shrimp. Cut deeply along the top ridge and rinse away the black vein, if present. Combine the cooking oil with the garlic and ginger in a small bowl and set aside.

Using a scissors, cut open the dried chiles and shake out the seeds. Discard the stems. Transfer the chiles to a bowl. Pour enough boiling water over the chiles to cover them. Put a small plate on top of the chiles so they are completely submerged and let soak for 30 minutes. Transfer the chiles to a blender. Add the tangerine juice, vinegar, brown sugar, and salt. Blend until completely liquefied. Peel the tangerines and separate the tangerine segments. Set the segments aside. The recipe can be prepared up to this point 8 hours ahead with the ingredients kept refrigerated in airtight containers.

When ready to cook, combine the cornstarch with 2 teaspoons cold water. Place a 12- to 14-inch frying pan over high heat. When the pan becomes hot, add the reserved garlic-oil mixture. When the garlic begins to brown, add the shrimp. Stir and toss until the shrimp turn white in the center (cut into a shrimp to check), about 3 minutes. Add the chile–tangerine juice mixture and the tangerine segments. Bring to a rapid boil and then stir in the cornstarch mixture.

Transfer to serving plates. Using a Microplane, grate a little nutmeg over the shrimp. Garnish with the chopped cilantro and serve at once.

GRILLED SWORDFISH *with* WATERMELON RELISH

SERVES 4

The key to this recipe is to purchase flawlessly fresh swordfish. If the swordfish is not at the peak of freshness or has been frozen, there will be a sea of disappointed faces at the dining table. It's easy to tell whether it's fresh. Look for the little spots, called the blood line. If the spots are red to pink, buy the swordfish. But if the blood line is gray, or the blood line has been trimmed away by the fishmonger, purchase another kind of firm-textured fresh fish.

4 (6- to 8-ounce) swordfish steaks

½ cup All-Purpose Marinade (page 28)

Watermelon Relish, for serving (page 21)

¼ cup crema

Prepare a dual-heat hot fire in a gas or charcoal grill.

Coat the swordfish on all sides with the marinade. Heat the watermelon relish to a simmer. Grill the swordfish over direct heat for about 2 minutes on each side or until lightly browned. Then slide the swordfish over to the "indirect side" of the grill, away from the heat. Cover the grill. Cook the swordfish for about 6 more minutes or until the fish is just cooked through (cut into the swordfish to check).

Transfer the swordfish to warm serving plates. Crown each piece of swordfish with a generous spoonful of the warm watermelon relish. Drizzle on some crema and serve at once.

There are a number of San Miguel streets perfect for the avid photographer.

PANFRIED FLOUNDER *with* PANKO AND POMEGRANATE MOLASSES

SERVES 4

This lovely recipe requires flawlessly fresh fish and confident enough cooking skills for all your guests to view as you storm into last-minute action. If pomegranates are available—they are in season in late fall and early winter—include some of the seeds as a garnish. The bright red seeds burst with flavor and have a wonderful crunchy texture. To remove the seeds from pomegranates, submerge a whole pomegranate in a bowl full of cold water and pull the pomegranate apart. Using your thumbs and forefingers (with everything still submerged) loosen the seeds. The seeds will sink to the bottom and the pomegranate shells will float to the top. Pomegranate seeds will keep for up to 2 weeks refrigerated.

4 (6-ounce) fresh flounder or catfish fillets

Salt and freshly ground black pepper

½ cup unbleached all-purpose flour

2 large eggs, well beaten

1 cup panko bread crumbs

POMEGRANATE SAUCE

½ cup low-sodium chicken broth

¼ cup pomegranate molasses, such as Carlo brand

3 tablespoons thin soy sauce

1 tablespoon hot sauce of your choice

2 tablespoons finely minced fresh ginger

2 tablespoons light brown sugar

2 teaspoons cornstarch

1 teaspoon ground cinnamon, preferably Mexican

1½ cups flavorless cooking oil

¼ cup chopped fresh cilantro, leaves and tender stems, or mint or basil leaves

¼ cup crumbled queso fresco

Pomegranate seeds, for garnish (optional)

Mariachi bands are often hired to add excitement to parties.

Lightly season the fish with salt and pepper on both sides. Place the flour on a dinner plate, the eggs in a shallow bowl, and the panko on another dinner plate. Coat the fish on both sides with flour. Dip each piece into the beaten egg to coat evenly, then into the panko to coat evenly. Place on a wire rack set over a baking sheet.

To make the pomegranate sauce, combine all of the ingredients in a small saucepan. The recipe can be prepared up to this point 8 hours before serving, with the sauce refrigerated in the saucepan. Do not cover the fish when refrigerating.

Place a 12-inch sauté pan over high heat. Add the cooking oil. Heat the oil until a piece of panko dropped into the oil bounces across the surface (or the end of a wooden spoon placed into the oil bubbles). Add 2 of the flounder pieces. Fry the fish until it turns golden on the underside. Gently turn over, and fry until golden on the second side, about 4 minutes total cooking. Drain on a wire rack. Fry the remaining 2 pieces the same way.

Transfer the fish to warm serving plates. Bring the pomegranate sauce to a simmer. Spoon the sauce over the fish. Garnish the flounder with the cilantro, queso fresco, and pomegranate seeds, if using. Serve at once.

LOBSTER *with* MEXICAN ACCENTS

SERVES 4

It is the Mango Salsa that contributes a Mexican flavor. If given a choice, choose lobster from the Atlantic coast. These are the only lobsters having the magnificent front claws packed with sweet-tasting meat. The other type of lobster, called spiny lobster, is captured along the coast from California to Chile, in Florida, throughout the South Pacific, and in the Mediterranean, and these don't have claws. Whatever type of lobster you buy, make a point to buy lobsters that have been newly pulled from the ocean, for their special flavor gradually dissipates the longer they are kept in a holding tank.

2 teaspoons salt

4 (2-pound) live lobsters

Mango Salsa or your favorite salsa, for serving (page 19)

Bring a large pot of water to a vigorous boil. Stir in the salt. Add the lobsters, head first, and then immediately cover the pot with its lid. Cook the lobsters until they turn bright red, about 8 minutes. Remove the lobsters from the boiling water.

To serve hot: When cool enough to handle, split the lobsters in half lengthwise using a sturdy kitchen knife or kitchen shears. Crack the claws with the dull edge of a sturdy knife or use a hammer! (It is less messy to cover the lobster with a clean kitchen towel—and then begin hammering!) Using paper towels, pull away and discard the green/purple liver. Serve with the mango salsa in small bowls alongside. Everyone cracks the claws and attacks with rolled-up sleeves.

To serve chilled: After pulling the lobsters out of the boiling water, transfer the lobsters to the sink or a large pot and cover the lobsters with crushed ice. Chill for 1 hour. Then split the lobsters in half lengthwise and crack the claws as directed. Discard the green/purple liver. If not serving right away, then refrigerate for up to 8 hours in advance. Accompany with the mango salsa in small bowls alongside.

MUSSELS *with* SALSA MEXICANA

SERVES 4

We'll hazard a guess that the vast majority of people who enthusiastically order mussels at restaurants never consider purchasing them at their favorite seafood counter. But mussels are so easy to cook and make a perfect choice for a weeknight dinner. Just buy the mussels the day of cooking. Be sure to buy mussels that are tightly closed, which is the key indicator of freshness. Then cook them in this delicious Mexican salsa. Serve with hot dinner rolls or slices of garlic bread.

3 pounds live mussels

4 cups Salsa Mexicana (page 17)

½ cup crumbled queso fresco

Scrub the mussels under cold running water and pull away the beards (a little seaweed-like attachment sometimes found at the edge of the shell). This can be done up to 6 hours ahead; place the mussels in a colander, cover with a wet towel, and refrigerate.

Place a 12- or 14-inch sauté pan over high heat. Add the salsa. When the salsa begins to boil, add the mussels. Cover tightly. When steam begins to escape between the lid and the pan, remove the lid. Give the mussels a stir—they should all have opened. If any do not open, discard these.

Transfer the mussels and salsa to deep soup bowls. Sprinkle with the crumbled queso fresco and serve at once. Accompany with hot dinner rolls or garlic bread.

Hugh Carpenter introducing recipes
at the beginning of class.

MEXICAN SEAFOOD RISOTTO

SERVES 6

This is one of our more complicated recipes and requires a lot of last-minute stirring. So don't undertake this on your own. Limit diners to six people, all of whom will be willing to take a turn stirring the rice. Start the evening with a couple of simple room temperature appetizers. Then everyone can assemble in the kitchen with a spoon in hand. Stir and stir, and stir again. Serve the seafood risotto as the main course, followed by a simple dinner salad, and then an outrageous chocolate dessert, perhaps contributed by one of the guests. In terms of seafood choices, this is excellent with fresh crabmeat, or large shrimp that are butterflied.

½ pound fresh chorizo sausage
(sold in links, not cured)

2 guajillo chiles

12 cups low-sodium chicken broth

4 cloves garlic, peeled

1 serrano chile, chopped,
including the seeds

¼ cup thinly sliced fresh
ginger, slices chopped

1 teaspoon black or tricolor peppercorns

2 teaspoons coriander seeds

1 teaspoon salt

½ teaspoon cumin seeds

1¼ pounds fresh salmon fillet,
skin and pinbones removed

1¼ pounds fresh bay or sea scallops

¼ cup olive oil

2 cups Arborio rice

1 cup dry white wine

½ cup chopped fresh cilantro,
leaves and tender stems, or basil
leaves, plus more for garnish

½ cup grated Parmigiano-Reggiano cheese

½ cup crema

Lime wedges, for serving

Squeeze the sausage meat out of the casings into a small bowl. Cut off the guajillo stems and shake out the seeds. Bring 4 cups of the chicken broth to a boil. Turn off the heat and add the chiles, submerging them with a small plate and soaking for 30 minutes. Then transfer the guajillo chiles and the broth they soaked in to a blender.

Heat a large heavy frying pan over high heat. Add the whole garlic cloves and serrano chile. Lightly blacken on two sides; then transfer to the blender. Add the ginger to the blender. In an electric spice grinder, place the pepper, coriander, salt, and cumin seeds. Grind to a fine powder, and then transfer the spices to the blender. Run the blender at high speed until everything is liquefied, about 30 seconds. Set aside.

Cut the salmon into 2-inch-long pieces that are about ¼ inch thick and 1 inch wide. If using sea scallops, pull off and discard the little secondary muscle if present; then cut the sea scallops into ¼-inch-wide slices. Combine the salmon and scallops in a bowl. The recipe can be prepared up to this point 12 hours in advance of cooking, with all food kept refrigerated in airtight containers.

Bring the remaining 8 cups chicken broth to a simmer in a large saucepan. Place a deep 14-inch sauté pan over medium-high heat. Add the ¼ cup olive oil. When hot, add the ground sausage. Cook until the sausage loses all of its raw color and breaks apart in little pieces.

Add the rice and sauté for 1 minute. Add the white wine and cook, constantly stirring, until all the wine is absorbed by the rice. Start adding the hot chicken broth, 2 cups at a time, and continue to stir until the liquid is absorbed. You do not have to stir constantly! Just give the rice a stir every 60 seconds. Add more broth each time as the broth is absorbed. When the rice still has a little raw texture and is still slightly brothy, after about 20 minutes of cooking, stir in half of the guajillo sauce. After the liquid is absorbed, stir in the remaining guajillo sauce. Taste. The rice should taste cooked but still slightly firm to the bite. Stir in the seafood and cook for about 5 minutes. Stir in the cilantro and Parmesan, then taste and adjust the salt, if necessary. (This is when you will have a debate with your other cooks!) Spoon into shallow bowls. Serve garnished with more cilantro, the crema, and lime wedges.

CHAPTER 8

Bold Mexican Flavors with
POULTRY AND MEAT

BBQ CHICKEN BREASTS *with* CORIANDER, CINNAMON, AND GARLIC

SERVES 4

This is a wonderful grilled chicken with all the intriguing flavors of Mexican cooking: sweet, sour, spicy, and smoky all united with plenty of chopped cilantro. From a cooking viewpoint, the challenge is to not overcook the chicken breasts. The solution is to first lightly brown the chicken by cooking the breasts directly over a medium-hot charcoal or gas grill, and then finish the cooking by moving the chicken away from direct heat, covering the grill, and cooking the chicken indirectly in a 300°F environment. Done in this manner, the chicken will be a marvel of tenderness. In order to ensure the correct temperature, use a combination instant-read meat-and-oven probe that has a cord attached to a little temperature monitor positioned next to the grill.

4 cloves garlic, minced

¼ cup chopped fresh cilantro, leaves and tender stems

3 tablespoons chipotle chiles in adobo sauce

¼ cup honey or lightly packed light brown sugar

¼ cup freshly squeezed lime juice

1 tablespoon ground coriander

1 teaspoon ground cinnamon, preferably Mexican

1 teaspoon salt

6 boneless, skin-on chicken breast halves

Flour or corn tortillas, warmed, for serving (see page 13)

Your choice of a salsa or guacamole, for serving

In a food processor, mince the garlic, then add the cilantro and mince again. Add the chiles, honey, lime juice, coriander, cinnamon, and salt. Process into a thick marinade.

Rub the marinade on both sides of the chicken breasts. Marinate for at least 15 minutes but ideally for 8 hours, refrigerated.

Prepare a medium-hot fire in a gas or charcoal grill. When hot, add the chicken. Sear the chicken on both sides until lightly browned, about 5 minutes. If using a gas grill, turn all burners off except one that is set on low, away from the chicken. If using a charcoal grill, move the chicken off the coals, and close the bottom and top vents 80 percent. Close the grill cover. Cook the chicken until the internal temperature reaches 155°F on an instant-read meat thermometer, about 20 minutes.

Warm the tortillas on the grill. Cut the chicken into slices. Serve the chicken with salsa or guacamole and warm tortillas.

BBQ CHICKEN *with* MEXICAN WALNUT SAUCE

SERVES 8

This recipe was inspired by a famous central Mexico dish, *chiles en nogada*, in which poblano chiles are stuffed with cooked chopped meat and fruit. It's served at room temperature with a walnut sauce having the colors of the Mexican flag: green (chopped cilantro), red (pomegranate seeds), and white (walnut cream sauce). It's a classic Mexican dish: multiple layers of flavor, vibrant color contrasts, and a lot of labor. This dish uses the same sauce, but as a finishing glaze on grilled chicken. It's a wonderful dish to serve at a dinner party. But it does require last-minute assembling, so you will need a couple of friends to help you plate and present the dish.

1 cup walnut halves, toasted

1½ cups low-sodium chicken broth

2 cloves garlic, cut into thirds

1 teaspoon salt

1 teaspoon freshly grated nutmeg

½ teaspoon ground cinnamon, preferably Mexican

¼ teaspoon cayenne pepper

½ cup heavy cream

½ cup crema

3 pounds boneless, skin-on chicken breasts

Salt and freshly ground black pepper

Olive oil, for brushing

2 teaspoons cornstarch (optional)

GARNISH

1 ripe avocado, sliced

½ cup pomegranate seeds or chopped red bell pepper

¼ cup chopped fresh cilantro, leaves and tender stems

8 lime wedges

Coarsely chop ½ cup walnuts and reserve.

In a blender, place the remaining ½ cup walnuts, the chicken broth, garlic, salt, nutmeg, cinnamon, and cayenne. Blend to liquefy. Transfer to a small saucepan. Stir in the cream and crema. The recipe can be prepared up to this point 24 hours ahead; refrigerate the chicken and sauce.

Prepare a medium dual fire in a gas or charcoal grill. Rub the chicken all over with salt, pepper, and olive oil. Refrigerate until ready to cook.

To cook, grill the breasts over direct heat until lightly browned on both sides, about 5 minutes. Then move the chicken away from direct heat. Cover the grill and cook the chicken until the internal temperature of the chicken is 155°F, about 20 minutes.

Heat the walnut sauce to a simmer over low heat. If you want a thicker sauce, stir in the cornstarch dissolved in 2 teaspoons cold water.

Slice the grilled chicken and transfer to warm serving plates. Spoon the walnut sauce over the meat and sprinkle with the reserved walnuts, pomegranate seeds, cilantro, and avocado slices. Serve at once accompanied by lime wedges.

BBQ CHICKEN *with* MOLE SAUCE

SERVES 8

Mole means "a mixture," and there are dozens of varieties of mole. The most famous are the red moles from Oaxaca and Puebla made with dried chiles and chocolate. Traditionally this took days to prepare and necessitated the laborious hand grinding (see the photo on page 64) of the chiles, along with as many as thirty additional ingredients (or more!), ground and added one by one. Now the electric blender has simplified the preparation, and mole sauces are everywhere. Usually the chicken or turkey is simmered in water until cooked, and then transferred to serving plates and topped with the mole sauce. But if the chicken is grilled, the dish has a more complex flavor and looks prettier on the plate. If you are serving this for a party of four instead of eight, don't try to adjust the quantity of mole sauce. The extra mole sauce will keep for 2 weeks, refrigerated. To use the sauce, bring it to a low boil, and then spoon it over any grilled (or roasted) meat or seafood.

MOLE SAUCE

3 ancho chiles, stemmed and seeded

3 guajillo chiles, stemmed and seeded

4 cups low-sodium chicken broth

6 cloves garlic, peeled

2 tablespoons white sesame seeds

4 medium vine-ripened tomatoes, quartered

1 tablespoon dried oregano, preferably Mexican

1 teaspoon ground cinnamon, preferably Mexican

1 teaspoon salt

¼ cup lightly packed light brown sugar

1 (750-milliliter) bottle inexpensive red wine, such as Cabernet Sauvignon or Zinfandel

2 ounces bittersweet chocolate, chopped

6 tablespoons Dry Rub #1 (page 26)

12 pieces chicken thighs, drumsticks, and breasts, 4 pounds

¼ cup olive oil

4 ounces queso fresco

¼ cup chopped fresh cilantro, leaves and tender stems, or parsley

3 limes, cut into wedges

Corn is highly regarded in the culture of Mexico.

To make the mole sauce, place the dried chiles in a large bowl. Bring the chicken broth to a boil and pour over the chiles. Place a plate on top of the chiles to submerge them, and soak for 30 minutes. Place a 12-inch frying pan over medium-high heat. When hot, toast the garlic until lightly browned. Toast the sesame seeds in the same frying pan until the sesame seeds become golden, about 3 minutes. In a blender, put the garlic, chiles, sesame seeds, and broth. Blend to liquefy. Add the tomatoes, oregano, cinnamon, and salt. Blend until extremely smooth. Transfer to a saucepan and add the brown sugar and red wine. Simmer over the lowest heat for 1 hour or until the liquid has reduced to 4 cups. Finely chop the chocolate and set this aside. The mole sauce can be made up to this point 1 week in advance and refrigerated in an airtight container.

Rub the dry rub on all sides of the chicken, then rub the chicken with the olive oil. Marinate the chicken for at least 1 hour, but for best results marinate 8 hours refrigerated. Prepare a gas or charcoal grill to medium heat. Grill the chicken until the internal temperature of the thighs reaches 165°F and the breasts reach 155°F. Turn the chicken every 3 to 5 minutes during grilling.

To serve, bring the mole sauce back to a simmer in a saucepan over low heat. Stir in the chocolate. Taste and adjust the seasonings as needed. Divide the sauce among serving plates. Place the grilled chicken on top of the sauce. Sprinkle with the queso fresco and chopped cilantro. Serve accompanied with lime wedges.

CHICKEN *with* GREEN MOLE SAUCE

SERVES 8

We use this green mole mostly with grilled or roasted meats and seafood. But it is also excellent as an appetizer dipping sauce for chilled shrimp or chunky jicama, or served cold in martini glasses or sake cups. It always delivers a flavor jolt.

2 poblano chiles

¼ cup pepitas (hulled pumpkin seeds)

3 tomatillos, papery skins removed

1 serrano chile (optional)

3 cloves garlic, peeled

2 cups low-sodium chicken broth

2 tablespoons light brown sugar

½ teaspoon salt

1 cup parsley sprigs, including some stems

1 cup packed spinach

1 cup fresh cilantro, leaves and tender stems

2 green onions, green part only

½ ripe avocado, pitted and peeled

2 frying chickens, cut into pieces, about 4 pounds

Salt and freshly ground black pepper

Olive oil, for brushing

1 cup crumbled queso fresco

3 limes, quartered

Roast the poblano chiles over a gas flame or in a dry cast-iron frying pan until charred. Place in a paper bag, seal, and let steam for 5 minutes. Using paper towels, rub off the charred skins. Seed and stem the chiles. Toast the pumpkin seeds in a frying pan over low heat, about 2 minutes. Let the seeds cool slightly and then grind to a powder using a spice grinder. In the same frying pan over high heat, add the tomatillos, serrano chile, if using, and garlic. Brown the serrano chile and garlic, about 5 minutes. Be sure to brown the tomatillos on both sides; this will take about 3 minutes per side.

In a blender, put the poblano chiles, pumpkin seeds, serrano chile, garlic, tomatillos, chicken broth, brown sugar, salt, parsley, spinach, cilantro, green onions, and avocado. Liquefy and then transfer to a large saucepan. Bring to a simmer, and cook for 5 minutes. Add salt to taste. This recipe can be done up to this point 8 hours in advance, with the chicken and mole sauce kept refrigerated.

Prepare a medium-hot fire in a gas or charcoal grill, or preheat the oven to 375°F. Rub the chicken all over with salt, pepper, and olive oil. Cover and set aside in the refrigerator until ready to cook. To cook the chicken, grill over medium heat until the internal temperature reaches 165°F for the thighs and 155°F for the breasts. If cooking in the oven, put the chicken on a baking sheet and roast in a 350°F oven for about 40 minutes.

Bring the green mole sauce to a simmer. Place the chicken pieces on serving plates and top with the green mole sauce. Garnish with the crumbled queso fresco and lime quarters.

GRILLED QUAIL *with* HIBISCUS SAUCE

SERVES 4

This fancy dish takes some planning and last-minute assembling. You'll need to order the fresh quail, boned, from the butcher at an upscale market such as Whole Foods. Fresh quail usually come six to a package. Please don't compromise on the quail. Fresh quail has a wonderful sweet taste totally absent from the frozen variety. Next you will need to locate dried hibiscus flowers. These are available at Mexican and Middle Eastern markets and at some health food stores. What's the reward for this effort? The dish is a fantastic combination of flavors, colors, and textures, the startling red sweet-sour-spicy sauce topped with the rich-tasting lightly charred quail. If you are stymied when it comes to locating the quail, substitute 4 boneless, skin-on chicken breasts. But for the hibiscus, there is no alternative.

HIBISCUS SAUCE

2 cups low-sodium chicken broth

1 cup dried hibiscus flowers

⅓ cup sugar

1 tablespoon Mexican chile sauce such as Cholula brand

2 tablespoons flavorless cooking oil

2 cloves garlic, minced

∽

8 boneless fresh quail, about 2 pounds

Your choice of Dry Rub (page 26)

¼ cup extra-virgin olive oil

2 teaspoons cornstarch

2 tablespoons unsalted butter, at room temperature

1 ripe avocado

¼ cup crema

¼ cup chopped fresh cilantro, leaves and tender stems

To make the sauce, bring the chicken broth to a boil in a small saucepan over medium heat. Turn off the heat and stir in the hibiscus flowers. Soak for 1 hour. Strain the broth into a bowl, discarding the hibiscus flowers. Stir the sugar and chile sauce into the hibiscus broth.

Place another medium saucepan over medium-high heat. Add the flavorless cooking oil. When hot, add the garlic. Stir the garlic until it begins to brown. Add the hibiscus broth. Bring to a boil, and cook over high heat until it is reduced to 1⅓ cups, about 5 minutes. Taste the sauce and adjust for sweet, sour, and spice. The sauce can be completed up to this point 24 hours in advance; let cool and then refrigerate in an airtight container.

Rub the quail all over with the dry rub, then rub with the olive oil. This can be completed up to 8 hours in advance, with the quail kept refrigerated.

Prepare a medium fire in a gas or charcoal grill. When ready to grill the quail, brush the grill grates with flavorless cooking oil and add the quail. Grill the quail for about 5 minutes on each side, keeping them moving, as they can easily stick to the grill. When just firm to the touch, about 150°F internal temperature, transfer the quail to a platter.

In San Miguel, the days of animal-drawn carts are not long past.

In a small saucepan, bring the hibiscus sauce to a low boil. Dissolve the cornstarch in 2 teaspoons cold water. Stir this a little at a time into the hibiscus sauce, adding only enough to slightly thicken the sauce. Remove the saucepan from the heat and stir in the butter.

To serve, pit, peel, and slice the avocado. Pour the hibiscus sauce onto warm serving plates. On each plate, position 2 grilled quail in the center of the sauce. Around the quail, place dots of the crema, a sprinkling of the cilantro, and 2 avocado slices per plate. Serve at once.

BBQ GAME HENS *in* MOJO SAUCE

SERVES 4

The complex flavors of this sauce will get everyone's mojo working at full speed. This recipe can be adapted to your taste. You can replace the game hens with boneless, skin-on chicken breasts, cooking them as described on page 121. Feel free to substitute a mix of fresh mint and basil for the cilantro. Or dress the game hens with one of the Zigzag Sauces on page 30.

MOJO SAUCE

8 cloves garlic, minced

¼ cup minced fresh ginger

½ bunch cilantro, leaves and tender stems, about 1 cup

2 teaspoons finely grated orange zest

2 cups freshly squeezed orange juice

3 tablespoons freshly squeezed lime juice

⅓ cup flavorless cooking oil

2 tablespoons sriracha chile sauce

2 tablespoons dark brown sugar

2 teaspoons dried oregano, preferably Mexican

2 teaspoons freshly ground black pepper

1 teaspoon salt

1 teaspoon ground cumin

1 teaspoon paprika

3 Rock Cornish game hens or small frying chickens, split in half (about 3 pounds)

1 teaspoon cornstarch

¼ cup crema

To make the sauce, combine the garlic, ginger, cilantro, orange zest, orange juice, lime juice, cooking oil, sriracha sauce, brown sugar, oregano, pepper, salt, cumin, and paprika in a medium bowl. Set aside 1 cup to use as a finishing sauce; the rest will be used as the marinade.

On each game hen, loosen a little bit of the breast skin. Spoon a couple of tablespoons of the mojo sauce between the skin and breast meat. Place the game hens in a large resealable plastic bag. Pour in the remaining marinade. Seal the bag and refrigerate for 4 to 8 hours.

To cook the hens, prepare a medium fire in a gas or charcoal grill. Grill the game hens until the internal temperature of the meat reaches 155°F. Turn the pieces over every few minutes. We like to close the grill for 5 minutes at a time, so the smoke flavors the game hens. During cooking, brush with some of the marinade from the plastic bag (but don't do this within the last 5 minutes of cooking time).

When cooked, transfer the game hens to warm serving plates. Pour the reserved mojo sauce into a small saucepan and bring to a boil. Meanwhile, dissolve the cornstarch in 1 teaspoon cold water. Stir in the cornstarch mixture to thicken the sauce. Spoon the mojo sauce over the game hens. Drizzle with the crema and serve.

BBQ BEEF *with* SPICY AVOCADO SAUCE

SERVES 4

The key is to use avocados that are at the peak of their season, such as the buttery Hass avocados grown along the coast of Southern California. We've also enjoyed the sauce with roasted or grilled chicken. Beef tenderloin can be expensive, so feel free to substitute your favorite steak, such as rib-eye, New York steak, or flat iron.

SPICY AVOCADO SAUCE

1 ripe avocado, pitted and peeled

¼ cup packed spinach

2 to 4 tablespoons cilantro sprigs, leaves and tender stems

1 tablespoon chopped fresh ginger

1 clove garlic, chopped

1 serrano chile, chopped, including the seeds

2 tablespoons freshly squeezed lime juice

1 teaspoon salt

1 cup low-sodium chicken broth, plus more as needed

4 (6- to 8-ounce) beef tenderloin steaks, trimmed by butcher of all silverskin

2 tablespoons of your choice of Dry Rub (page 26)

¼ cup olive oil

GARNISH

1 red bell pepper, chopped

½ cup crumbled queso fresco or crema

To prepare the sauce, place the flesh from the avocado into a blender. Add the spinach, cilantro, ginger, garlic, serrano chile, lime juice, salt, and broth. Process the mixture until liquefied. Taste and adjust the flavors, if needed. If the sauce is too thick, thin by stirring in extra chicken broth. Transfer to a small saucepan. The sauce can be completed up to this point 24 hours in advance and refrigerated in an airtight container.

Prepare a medium-hot fire in a gas or charcoal grill. Rub the steaks on both sides with the dry rub, then rub with the olive oil. To cook the steaks, brush the grill grates with oil. Add the steaks and grill to the desired doneness (for medium-rare, about 10 minutes, and about 124°F on a meat thermometer).

Warm the avocado sauce over low heat on the stovetop. Pour the avocado sauce onto warm serving plates. Place the steaks in the center of the sauce. Garnish with the diced red bell pepper and queso fresco. Serve at once.

BBQ BEEF *with* MANGO-CHILE SAUCE

SERVES 4

There are lots of bright, exciting flavors in this easy-to-make recipe. If ripe mango is not available, substitute papaya. Plan a Mexican fiesta. A good menu might be this dish plus Marinated Goat Cheese with Chiles and Mint (page 38), Chilled Avocado Soup (page 94), Oven Fries Olé Olé! (page 157), Yellow Watermelon Salad (page 77), and Coconut Ice Cream (page 169). Or act the role of a party planner and ask your cooking friends to each bring a recipe ready to serve or to cook. Then sit back and relax!

MANGO SAUCE

1 cup chopped mango

2 tablespoons minced fresh ginger

2 cloves garlic, minced

1 serrano chile, minced, including the seeds

½ cup low-sodium chicken broth

2 tablespoons freshly squeezed lime juice

2 tablespoons light brown sugar

½ teaspoon salt

½ teaspoon ground allspice or cinnamon (preferably Mexican) or freshly grated nutmeg

¼ cup chopped fresh cilantro, leaves and tender stems, or mint leaves

4 (6- to 8-ounce) beef tenderloin steaks, trimmed by the butcher of all silverskin, or your favorite steak

2 tablespoons of your choice of Dry Rub (page 26)

Olive oil, for brushing

To make the mango sauce, place the mango, ginger, garlic, chile, broth, lime juice, brown sugar, salt, and allspice in a blender. Puree until smooth. Transfer to a small saucepan and add the cilantro. Taste and adjust the seasonings if needed. The sauce can be made 12 hours ahead and kept refrigerated in an airtight container.

Rub the meat with the dry rub, then rub with the olive oil. Marinate anywhere from a few minutes to 8 hours. If marinating for more than 30 minutes, refrigerate the meat. When ready to grill the steaks, prepare a hot fire in a gas or charcoal grill. Grill the steaks to your desired doneness (about 125°F for medium-rare). We prefer to sear the steaks over direct high heat, and then after they are charred (about 6 minutes), move the steaks away from direct heat, and finish cooking indirectly with the grill covered.

Transfer the steaks to warm serving plates. Bring the mango sauce to a simmer on the stovetop. Spoon the mango sauce over the meat and serve at once.

BBQ STEAK CASCABEL

SERVES 4

Cascabel means "rattle," and indeed, the seeds cause a rattling sound when the chile is shaken. These chiles are thick-fleshed, medium hot, and slightly smoky in flavor. If you can't find the cascabel chiles, substitute two ancho chiles. This sauce is very versatile. It's good spooned onto grilled jumbo shrimp or chicken hot off the grill. It also makes a great shrimp cocktail sauce in martini glasses with chilled cooked shrimp perched around the rim.

CASCABEL SAUCE

3 cascabel chiles

2 guajillo chiles

2 cups freshly squeezed orange juice

¼ cup red or white wine vinegar

¼ cup lightly packed brown sugar

¾ teaspoon salt

¼ cup extra-virgin olive oil, divided

2 large cloves garlic, minced

4 (6- to 8-ounce) steaks of your choice, such as rib-eye, New York, or beef tenderloin

2 tablespoons your choice of Dry Rub (page 26)

1 whole nutmeg

¼ cup chopped fresh cilantro, leaves and tender stems, or parsley

To make the sauce, bring 4 cups water to a boil. Use scissors to cut open the dried chiles and shake out the seeds. Discard the stem area. Transfer the chiles to a heatproof bowl and pour the boiling water over the chiles. Put a small plate on top of the chiles so they are completely submerged, and soak for 30 minutes. Remove the chiles from the soaking water and transfer the chiles to a blender. Add the orange juice, vinegar, brown sugar, and salt. Blend until completely liquefied.

Place a 10-inch frying pan over high heat. Add the garlic and half the olive oil. When the garlic begins to brown, add the chile–orange juice mixture. Bring to a rapid boil, and boil until reduced to 1¼ cups. The sauce can be made 24 hours in advance, transferred to a small saucepan, and refrigerated.

Sprinkle the dry rub on both sides of the steaks, then rub it vigorously onto the surface of the steaks. Rub the steaks on both sides with 2 tablespoons of the olive oil.

Meanwhile, prepare a hot fire in a gas or charcoal grill. Grill the steaks to the desired degree of doneness (125°F for medium-rare).

Bring the sauce to a low boil. Taste and adjust the seasonings if needed. Place the steaks on warm serving plates. Top with the chile-orange sauce. Use a Microplane to grate a little nutmeg over the steak and sauce. Garnish with the chopped cilantro and serve at once.

GRILLED FLATIRON STEAK
with TANGERINE SALSA

SERVES 4

Flatiron is our favorite steak. Shaped like flank steak, but about half the size, it is from the top of the shoulder. Well-marbled flatiron steak has a slight "chew" similar to New York steak and a superb beef flavor that lingers long after the last bite. If you don't see flatiron steak at your market, place an order with the butcher. In the meantime, choose your favorite steak. Cooked on a hot fire, it will taste fantastic topped with this salsa featuring tangerine segments. Please note to make this recipe only when tangerines are in season. Orange segments are larger, fleshier, and do not make a good substitute.

2 pounds flatiron steak or your favorite steak

2 tablespoons tricolor peppercorns, coarsely ground

¼ cup mushroom soy sauce or Worcestershire sauce

Tangerine-Serrano Salsa (page 20), at room temperature

Rub the steaks on both sides with the ground pepper. Then rub the steaks with the soy sauce.

Prepare a hot fire in a gas or charcoal grill. When hot, brush the grill grates with oil. Grill the steaks for about 4 minutes on each side, until medium-rare in the center (about 125°F on an instant-read meat thermometer). Let the meat rest for 6 minutes off the grill.

Cut the steak crosswise against the grain into ½-inch-thick slices. Transfer the slices to warm serving plates. Stir the salsa and spoon the salsa on top of the steaks. Serve at once.

BRAISED VEAL SHANKS, VERACRUZ-STYLE

SERVES 4

The combination of tomatoes and olives is common in Veracruz yet rarely appears on the menus of Mexican restaurants north of the border. It is most commonly used on grilled fish, but the sauce is also terrific as a braising liquid for veal shanks. In this recipe, we introduce an unusual technique. Instead of dusting the shanks with flour and browning them in a pan, the shanks are browned on a grill and then braised in the sauce. This extra step gives the dish a more complex taste. If veal shanks are unavailable, substitute 8 skinned chicken thighs, or 2 pounds pork shoulder cut into 2-inch cubes, or 4 pounds beef short ribs on the bone.

4 veal shanks, cut by the butcher into 2-inch-thick pieces

2 tablespoons of your choice of Dry Rub (page 26)

¼ cup olive oil, plus more for veal shanks

3 cloves garlic, minced

2 cups chopped vine-ripened tomatoes

2 cups low-sodium chicken broth

½ teaspoon ground allspice

½ teaspoon salt

1 cinnamon stick, preferably Mexican

1 serrano chile, minced, including the seeds (optional)

½ cup chopped imported green or black olives (not canned)

¼ cup chopped fresh parsley

1 whole green onion, chopped

1 tablespoon cornstarch

Finely grated zest of 1 lime

Finely grated zest of 1 orange

Prepare a medium-hot fire in a gas or charcoal grill. Preheat the oven to 325°F.

Rub the shanks with the dry rub. Rub with the olive oil. Place the shanks on the grill and cook the shanks on both sides until evenly browned but not blackened.

Add the ¼ cup olive oil to a deep 8-quart ovenproof pot with a lid. Add the garlic and lightly brown over low heat. Add the tomatoes, broth, allspice, salt, cinnamon, chile, if using, olives, parsley, and green onion. Stir to evenly mix. Bring to a simmer, then add the veal shanks to the sauce.

Cover the pot and transfer the shanks to the oven. Cook until the veal shanks are tender, about 1½ hours. The shanks can be done up to this point 24 hours in advance, with the veal shanks and sauce refrigerated together in the pot.

To serve, if the veal has been chilled, scrape off all hardened fat that has formed on the surface. If the dish has not been chilled, then blot up any oil floating on the surface with paper towels. Heat the veal shanks on the stovetop until they are piping hot. Taste and sauce and adjust the seasonings, especially for salt.

Many Indian conversion chapels are open for visiting in the countryside. You can tour them by horseback or four-wheel drive.

Transfer the veal shanks to warm serving plates. Bring the sauce to a low boil. If the sauce seems thin, mix 1 tablespoon cornstarch with an equal amount of cold water and stir into the sauce little by little. Ladle the sauce over the shanks. Sprinkle with the grated lime and orange zests. Serve at once.

BBQ PORK *in* YUCATÁN ACHIOTE SAUCE

SERVES 4

To learn about the essential ingredient in this dish, achiote paste, see page 9. There is no substitute for this complex, curry paste–like ingredient. Sold in brightly colored 3½-ounce boxes, achiote paste will keep for two years stored in the pantry. Press the box with your fingers. It should feel slightly soft to the touch. This sauce has a wonderful complex flavor. For a variation, spoon it onto heated serving plates and top with grilled jumbo shrimp, chicken thighs and breasts, or grilled steak.

YUCATÁN ACHIOTE SAUCE

1 ancho chile

2 cups low-sodium chicken broth

2 ounces achiote paste

1 cup freshly squeezed orange juice

2 tablespoons light brown sugar

1 tablespoon chopped fresh oregano, preferably Mexican

½ teaspoon salt

4 cloves garlic, chopped

2 tablespoons vegetable or olive oil

1 (1½-inch) cinnamon stick, preferably Mexican

2 pork tenderloins or 4 chicken breast halves (about 2 pounds)

1 teaspoon ground cumin

1 teaspoon ground coriander

1 teaspoon freshly ground black pepper

3 tablespoons extra-virgin olive oil

GARNISH

1 to 2 limes, cut into wedges

½ cup chopped fresh parsley or cilantro, leaves and tender stems

1 ripe avocado

continued on next page

Vintage garden fountains can still be seen at ranchos outside of town.

To make the sauce, stem and seed the ancho chile. Place the chile in a medium heatproof bowl. Bring the chicken broth to a boil, and then pour over the chile. Submerge the chile using a small plate and soak for 30 minutes. Remove the chile from the soaking water and transfer the chile and soaking liquid to a blender. Add the achiote paste, orange juice, brown sugar, oregano, and salt. Blend until completely liquefied.

Place in a 10-inch frying pan over high heat. Add the garlic and olive oil. When the garlic begins to brown, add the cinnamon stick, and chile–orange juice mixture. Bring to a rapid boil, and boil until reduced to 1¼ cups. Discard the cinnamon stick. The sauce can be made 24 hours in advance, transferred to a small saucepan, and refrigerated.

Within 8 hours of cooking, rub the pork with the cumin, coriander, and black pepper. Then rub with the oil. Refrigerate if done more than 30 minutes prior to cooking. Meanwhile, prepare a medium-hot fire in a gas or charcoal grill, or preheat the oven to 400°F.

Grill the pork to an internal temperature of 142°F, or the chicken to an internal temperature of 155°F. Alternatively in a 325°F oven, roast the pork or chicken for approximately 30 minutes.

Pit, peel, and slice the avocado. Bring the achiote sauce back to a simmer, if necessary. Taste and adjust the seasonings if needed. Spoon the sauce onto warm serving plates. You will have extra sauce! Slice the pork and place on top of the sauce; or place the chicken breasts whole on top of the sauce. Garnish with the lime wedges, parsley, and avocado.

CHIPOTLE-BRAISED LAMB SHANKS

SERVES 4

As with most stews, this dish tastes better if made a day before serving. You've got the advantage, too, of being able to lift off the hard layer of fat that forms on the top surface after the stew chills. For a variation, substitute veal shanks, bone-in chicken thighs, or 2-inch cubes of pork shoulder.

4 pounds lamb shanks, cut by the butcher into 2-inch-thick pieces

3 tablespoons of your choice of Dry Rub (page 26)

½ cup unbleached all-purpose flour

¼ cup extra-virgin olive oil

1 medium yellow onion, peeled and chopped into ½-inch dice

4 cloves garlic, minced

2 cups chopped vine-ripened tomatoes, including seeds

1 cup dry red wine or low-sodium chicken broth

2 tablespoons chipotle chiles in adobo sauce, minced

1 tablespoon tomato paste from a tube

1 bay leaf

1 chopped fresh oregano, preferably Mexican

¾ teaspoon salt

½ cup crumbled queso fresco or crema

¼ cup chopped fresh parsley

2 limes, cut into wedges

Preheat the oven to 325°F. Rub the shanks with the dry rub, then coat lightly with the flour. Place a large ovenproof pot with a lid over medium heat. When hot, add the olive oil. When the oil becomes hot, add the onion. Turn the heat to low and cook the onion until it caramelizes, about 15 minutes, stirring occasionally.

Remove the onion and set aside. If the surface of the pan is dry, add a few more tablespoons of olive oil. Turn the heat to medium-high and add the shanks. Brown the shanks on all sides, 6 to 8 minutes. Add the garlic. Push the garlic down between the shanks to make sure they touch the bottom of the pan. Cook until most of the garlic has just begun to brown, about 1 minute.

Meanwhile, in a medium bowl, combine the cooked onion, tomatoes, wine, chipotle chiles, tomato paste, bay leaf, oregano, and salt. Pour this mixture around the shanks. Bring to a low boil, then cover the pot and transfer to the oven. Cook until the meat easily pulls away from the bone when prodded with a fork, about 2 hours. Midway through the cooking, turn the shanks over. The shanks can be made up to this point 2 days in advance and refrigerated in the pot.

To serve, remove the layer of hardened fat on top of the stew. Or, if you have not refrigerated it, then dab up the surface fat using paper towels. Bring the stew to a simmer. Transfer the shanks and sauce to warm serving plates. Sprinkle with the crumbled queso fresco and chopped parsley. Serve at once with the lime wedges on the side.

ROAST RACK OF LAMB *with* COFFEE, CHILES, AND CHOCOLATE

SERVES 4

This recipe takes the favorite Mexican seasonings of coffee, cinnamon, cayenne, chocolate, and cilantro and uses them to augment the flavor of grilled racks of lamb. There are layers and layers of complex flavors in this dish, so choose a menu of milder dishes to accompany it, such as Saffron Rice Pilaf (page 151) and Grilled Vegetables (page 159).

2 racks of lamb, trimmed and cut by the butcher into double-rib pieces (you will have 8 pieces)

2 tablespoons Dry Rub #1 (page 26)

2 teaspoons espresso powder

2 to 3 tablespoons olive oil

1 cup strong brewed coffee

½ cup heavy cream

1 clove garlic, minced

2 teaspoons cornstarch

½ teaspoon salt

½ teaspoon ground cinnamon, preferably Mexican

¼ teaspoon ground cayenne pepper

¼ cup finely chopped bittersweet chocolate

¼ cup chopped fresh cilantro, leaves and tender stems

¼ cup crumbled queso fresco

Trim any excess fat from the chops. Rub the meat with the dry rub, then with the espresso powder, and finally with the olive oil.

In a small saucepan, combine the coffee, cream, garlic, cornstarch, salt, cinnamon, and cayenne. The recipe can be prepared up to this point 24 hours in advance, with all food refrigerated.

Preheat the oven to 400°F. Place the lamb on a rimmed baking sheet, and roast in the oven until the internal temperature registers 130°F on an instant-read meat thermometer, about 20 minutes depending on the size of the racks.

Stir the sauce, then bring to a low boil. Turn off the heat. Stir in the chocolate and 2 tablespoons of the cilantro. Place the lamb on warm serving plates. Pour the sauce over the lamb. (Or pour the sauce onto each plate, and then center the lamb on top of the sauce.) Sprinkle with the remaining 2 tablespoons cilantro and the queso fresco and serve at once.

MEXICAN CHILI *with* LAMB AND BLACK BEANS
SERVES 8

Lots of goat is eaten in Mexico but very little lamb. Yet lamb is a perfect canvas for the aggressive seasonings of Mexican cuisine. Don't be alarmed by the daunting list of ingredients here. After soaking the chiles and toasting the garlic, onion, and serrano, the recipe is quickly finished in a blender. The complex flavors of this dish intensify when it is made a day in advance.

2 cups dried black beans

2 ancho chiles

2 guajillo chiles

6 cups low-sodium chicken broth, plus more if needed

¼ cup flavorless cooking oil

1 medium yellow onion, diced

10 cloves garlic, chopped

1½ pounds ground lamb

8 medium vine-ripened tomatoes

1 tablespoon chopped fresh oregano, preferably Mexican

1 tablespoon chopped fresh thyme

2 serrano chiles, chopped, including the seeds

1 tablespoon achiote paste

1 teaspoon salt

1 teaspoon freshly ground black pepper

1 teaspoon ground cumin

½ teaspoon ground cinnamon, preferably Mexican

½ teaspoon ground cloves

¼ cup lightly packed light brown sugar

4 ears white corn, shucked

Crema, for drizzling

¼ cup coarsely chopped fresh cilantro, leaves and tender stems

One of many Indian conversion chapels in the countryside.

Spread the black beans on a dinner plate, and pick through the beans, removing any pebbles. In a small bowl, cover the black beans with cold water. Soak the black beans overnight. Drain the beans.

Cut the stems off the ancho and guajillo chiles. Cut in half, and shake away all the seeds. Put them in a medium heatproof bowl. Bring the chicken broth to a boil, and then pour over the chiles in the bowl. Place a small plate on top of the chiles to submerge them. Soak for 30 minutes.

Meanwhile, place the cooking oil in a 3-quart saucepan over medium heat. Add the onion and cook, stirring occasionally, until brown, about 10 minutes. Add the garlic and cook until lightly golden, about 2 minutes. Add the lamb. Stir the lamb to break it apart and cook it until it loses all its raw color.

Coarsely chop 4 of the tomatoes, including the seeds. Stir the tomatoes into the lamb. Cut the remaining 4 tomatoes into quarters and put into a blender. Add the rehydrated chiles and chicken broth, oregano, thyme, serrano chiles, achiote, salt, pepper, cumin, cinnamon, cloves, and brown sugar to the blender and blend until liquefied.

Pour this blended mixture into the saucepan holding the lamb. Stir in the black beans. Bring to a simmer, and simmer constantly for 1½ hours. The chili can be done up to this point 2 days ahead, with the chili refrigerated in the pot in which it was cooked.

Cut the corn kernels off the cobs. Bring the chili to a simmer. Taste the chili, adding more salt if necessary. And taste the beans; they should be very tender. Stir in the corn. Cook the chili for 5 minutes. Taste and adjust the seasonings if needed. Ladle the chili into bowls and drizzle with the crema and chopped cilantro. Serve at once.

PULLED PORK *with* CHILES, ORANGE, AND CILANTRO

SERVES 4

This delicious recipe takes time and special equipment. You'll need a smoker such as a Big Green Egg or a Komodo Kamado and an electronic meat probe attached to a screen that will display the internal temperature of the meat, a small wire rack, and a pizza stone to act as a heat diffuser. There are lots of recipes on the Internet providing directions for making pulled pork in a slow cooker or oven. But smoking is the only way to achieve the true smoky flavors that are the essence of this dish. Serve the pork as soft tacos or tostados, or as the filling for chiles rellenos. Note that despite the names, pork "shoulder" and "butt" are the same cut of meat.

3½ pounds pork shoulder/butt

2 tablespoons of your choice
of Dry Rub (page 26)

¼ cup olive oil

CHILE-ORANGE MOP

1 tablespoon finely grated orange zest

½ cup freshly squeezed orange juice

¼ cup thin soy sauce

¼ cup vinegar, any type

¼ cup extra-virgin olive oil

¼ cup honey

¼ cup minced chipotle
chiles in adobo sauce

¼ cup minced fresh ginger

6 cloves garlic, minced

2 whole green onions, minced

¼ cup chopped fresh cilantro,
leaves and tender stems

FOR SERVING

Flour or corn tortillas

Your choice of salsa (pages 17–20)

Guacamole (page 16)

Your choice of Zigzag Sauce (page 30)

Rub the pork vigorously with the dry rub. Then rub all over with the olive oil. Bring the meat to room temperature.

To make the chile-orange mop, combine all of the ingredients in a medium bowl.

Prepare a 250°F fire in a barbecue smoker. Place a heat-diffusing stone in the smoker. Line a small baking pan with aluminum foil and spray the foil with nonstick cooking spray. Also spray a small wire rack on both sides. Place the baking pan in the smoker, add the wire rack, and then place the meat on the rack. Close the lid of the smoker, and cook the meat until the internal temperature reaches 160°F, about 4 hours (observing the rise of temperature on the digital screen of the meat thermometer). Do not open the smoker! At this point, the meat will still be very tough.

Lay a large sheet of aluminum foil on the counter. Gently transfer the meat to the foil, positioning it so that it is stable. Bring the foil up around the sides of the meat so that the meat is resting in a foil bowl. Brush the meat with the chile-orange mop, and pour the rest of the mop into the foil bowl. Close the top of the foil package (completely sealed but not tightly wrapped!). Insert the temperature gauge through the foil and deep into the meat. As described in the headnote, the meat thermometer should be the kind attached by a cord to a temperature screen. Gently return the meat to the smoker (you can place it on the rack or directly on the stone). Cook until the internal temperature reaches 190°F, about 1½ hours more.

Carefully remove the foil package from the smoker, and even more carefully open the foil to let the steam escape. Pour the mop into a small saucepan or bowl. Using paper towels, soak up the fat. Let the meat cool on the foil for 1 hour.

Preheat the oven to 325°F. Use forks to pull the meat into shreds; the meat should be so tender that it falls apart with just the lightest prodding with a fork. Place in a baking dish and pour the mop over the meat. You will have approximately 6 cups of shredded meat and 1 cup of the mop. The pork can be prepared and kept warm in the oven for 1 hour, or stored, refrigerated, up to 2 days before serving, with the pork still moistened by the Chile-Orange Mop in an airtight container.

To serve, cover the meat and warm it in the oven until hot. Drain away the Chile-Orange Mop. Warm the tortillas (see page 13). Serve the pork with the warm tortillas, salsa, guacamole, and a zigzag sauce.

CHAPTER 9

EASY SIDE DISHES
with Mexican Flavors

MEXICAN RICE PILAF

SERVES 4

Mexican cooks add their own twist to rice cooked pilaf style. The raw rice is given the typical careful rinsing in order to remove the gluten and starch. It's then cooked in a little vegetable oil. But whereas Europeans give the rice just a minute or two of preliminary sautéing, Mexican cooks sauté the rice for about 10 minutes, until it nearly becomes browned. Also, a few chopped tomatoes are added to give the rice a lovely color. In this recipe, we add a serrano chile when sautéing the rice, and then remove it, leaving behind a shadow of its heat.

1½ cups long-grain white rice

3 tablespoons flavorless cooking oil

2 cloves garlic, minced

1 serrano chile, split open lengthwise and seeds removed

1 cup chopped vine-ripened tomatoes including the seeds

3 cups low-sodium chicken broth

½ teaspoon salt

Place the rice in a sieve and rinse under cold running water, rubbing the rice with your fingers until the water is no longer cloudy, about 2 minutes. Drain thoroughly.

Place a 3-quart saucepan over medium-high heat. Add the oil and garlic. After 15 seconds, add the rice and serrano chile. Turn the heat to low, and sauté the rice for 5 to 10 minutes. Remove the serrano chile. Add the tomatoes, broth, and salt. Bring to a low boil, stirring. Cover, lower the heat to the lowest setting, and simmer for 20 minutes, never lifting the cover.

Taste the rice. If it is still slightly undercooked, cover the saucepan, and simmer for another 5 minutes. The rice can be made up to this point 24 hours ahead, with the rice refrigerated in the saucepan in which it cooked, lid on. Return to room temperature and reheat in a 300°F oven for 30 minutes.

Left, a painting of St. John the Baptist in an old chapel. Right, twilight in San Miguel when the street lamps are lighted.

Variations

COCONUT RICE PILAF

Coconut milk contributes a rich lingering flavor and intensifies the white rice color. Other types of long-grain rice that can be substituted are Thai jasmine rice and basmati rice. We've also varied the recipe by replacing the rice with the same amount of Israeli couscous—excellent!

Prepare the rice pilaf recipe as directed, but use 1 cup coconut milk and 2½ cups chicken broth instead of the 3 cups chicken broth. Proceed as directed.

SAFFRON RICE PILAF

Imagine having to pick 14,000 crocus stigmas to yield 1 ounce of saffron! No wonder it's the world's most expensive spice. Of course, there is inexpensive powdered saffron, but then the pilaf will not have the startling yellow color, or the elusive aroma, or the beautiful yellow-scarlet threads scattered throughout the dish. Saffron threads are sold in the spice section of most supermarkets.

Prepare the rice pilaf as directed. When adding the chicken broth, add one big pinch saffron. Finish as directed.

MEXICAN RICE VERDE

SERVES 8

This complex-tasting and green-tinted rice gains its flavor from spinach, cilantro, mint, serrano chiles, and orange zest. We love serving it with grilled or roasted halibut because of the dramatic color variation.

1½ cups long-grain white rice

3 cups low-sodium chicken broth

½ teaspoon salt

1 cup firmly packed spinach

½ cup fresh cilantro, leaves and tender stems

½ cup fresh mint leaves

½ serrano chile, including the seeds (optional)

½ teaspoon finely grated orange zest

3 tablespoons flavorless cooking oil or unsalted butter

1 tablespoon minced fresh ginger

3 cloves garlic, minced

Place the rice in a colander and rinse until the rice water is no longer cloudy, about 2 minutes.

Place the chicken broth, salt, spinach, cilantro, mint, serrano chile, if using, and orange zest in a blender. Liquefy, then set aside. This can be made up to this point 12 hours ahead of cooking, stored and refrigerated in an airtight container.

Place a 2½-quart saucepan over medium heat. Add the cooking oil. When hot, add the rice, ginger, and garlic. Sauté for 5 minutes, stirring occasionally.

Add the reserved broth mixture. Bring to a low boil. Cover, and cook the rice for 20 minutes, never lifting the lid. After 20 minutes, taste the rice. If not fully cooked, cover the pot and cook for another 5 minutes before tasting the rice again. The rice can be made ahead and refrigerated in its pot. Return to room temperature, and reheat in a 300°F oven for 30 minutes.

Clockwise from top left: The Indian pyramid site just outside of town, called Cañada de la Virgen. A conversion chapel. A cornfield plowed by animals in preparation for the summer rains. An altar inside a country church maintained by the locals. Glorious colors decorate a country church. Barrel cactus are native to the area.

MEXICAN WILD RICE

SERVES 4

It's the corn, cilantro, and pumpkin seeds that contribute a Mexican flavor to this dish. For a great variation, add ½ teaspoon ground cumin or Mexican cinnamon at the same time you stir in the currants.

1 cup wild rice

4 tablespoons unsalted butter

3 cloves garlic, minced

½ cup minced green onion, green and white parts

3 ears white sweet corn, kernels cut off cob

½ cup dried currants or raisins

1 cup low-sodium chicken broth

1 teaspoon finely grated orange zest

¼ cup fresh cilantro, leaves and tender stems, chopped

½ cup toasted pepitas (hulled pumpkin seeds; page 12)

½ teaspoon salt

Cook the wild rice according to the directions on the package. This can be done up to 24 hours in advance; refrigerate the rice.

Place a 12-inch sauté pan over medium-high heat. Melt the butter, and sauté the garlic for a few seconds. Add the cooked wild rice and cook, stirring, until heated through, about 5 minutes. During cooking, stir in the green onion, corn, currants, chicken broth, and grated orange zest. Bring to a low boil, stirring occasionally. Cook until all the moisture disappears and the wild rice sizzles in the pan. Stir in the cilantro and pumpkin seeds and serve. You can make this up to 12 hours ahead; reheat in a 300°F oven for 20 minutes.

The agave cactus has played an important role in the history and culture of San Miguel.

CORN BREAD MUFFINS SPECKLED *with* ROASTED RED PEPPER

SERVES 4 TO 6

The cooking directions provide two options, a cast-iron muffin pan or a cast-iron skillet. We prefer the muffin pan because more of the surface becomes crisp and because it is easier to reheat individual muffins. Serve with grilled meat or seafood that has an accompanying sauce that begs to be sopped up.

1½ cups yellow cornmeal

½ cup unbleached all-purpose flour

2 teaspoons baking powder

1 teaspoon salt

3 large eggs, well beaten

1¼ cups buttermilk or whole milk

⅓ cup unsalted butter, melted, plus 1 tablespoon for buttering the pan

¼ cup honey

6 ounces bottled roasted red pepper, chopped

3 ears white sweet corn, kernels cut off cob

¼ cup chopped fresh cilantro, leaves and tender stems

3 cloves garlic, minced

Preheat the oven to 400°F. In a large bowl, place the cornmeal, flour, baking powder, and salt. Mix well. In a separate bowl, combine the eggs, buttermilk, butter, and honey. Mix well. Add the chopped roasted red pepper, corn kernels, cilantro, and garlic to the buttermilk mixture. Mix well. Then stir this into the cornmeal mixture. Stir until the dry ingredients are barely moistened, leaving plenty of lumps.

Butter a 6-cup cast-iron muffin pan or 10-inch cast-iron skillet and preheat for 15 minutes in the oven. When heated, pour in the batter. Bake for about 10 minutes if using a muffin pan, or 30 minutes in the skillet. The corn bread is done when a knife pushed deep into the center comes out clean. If cooked in the skillet, cut the corn bread into slices.

To serve, place in a basket lined with a cloth napkin, cover, and warm in a 225°F oven. Serve with butter and honey.

GARLIC BREAD SCENTED *with* CUMIN

SERVES 4

Here's garlic bread with a slight south-of-the-border taste. Choose a good country-style loaf of white bread, with a firm texture and very few "canyons" in the bread.

½ cup unsalted butter

8 cloves garlic, minced

1 bunch chives, minced

¼ cup chopped fresh cilantro, leaves and tender stems

½ teaspoon ground cumin (optional)

Freshly ground black pepper

1 (12-inch) loaf French bread

½ cup grated Parmigiano-Reggiano cheese

Preheat the broiler, or prepare a hot fire in a gas or charcoal grill.

In a small saucepan, place the butter, garlic, chives, cilantro, cumin, if using, and black pepper to taste. Melt the butter over low heat until it bubbles around the edges of the pan. Remove from the heat.

Split the bread in half horizontally. Brush on a thin layer of the butter sauce. If broiling the bread, sprinkle on the cheese. If grilling the bread, set the cheese aside. This can be done 12 hours before cooking; seal the bread in a paper or plastic bag.

Toast the bread under the broiler until golden, about 3 minutes. If grilling the bread, toast the bread cut side down. When toasted, turn the bread over and sprinkle on the cheese. Continue cooking until lightly browned on the underside. Cut into slices and serve.

OVEN FRIES OLÉ OLÉ!

SERVES 4

This easy recipe is an excellent side dish for any of the main courses in this book. It is also very good made with garnet yams, peeled to reveal the bright orange interior, and then cut in the same manner as the russet potatoes.

3 medium russet potatoes,
or 16 small round red potatoes

4 cloves garlic, minced

Generous pinch of ancho or
chipotle chile powder

½ teaspoon salt

Freshly ground black pepper

¼ cup extra-virgin olive oil

Preheat the oven to 425°F. Line a baking pan with aluminum foil. Spray the foil with nonstick cooking spray.

Cut the russet potatoes in half lengthwise, then cut each half lengthwise into 3 strips. (If using red potatoes, cut them in half.) Place in a bowl. Add the garlic, chile powder, salt, and black pepper to taste. Toss to evenly season, then add the olive oil, and toss again. The potatoes can be prepared up to this point 4 hours before cooking.

Scatter the potatoes onto the baking pan, and turn each piece to be resting on the skin side. Roast until tender when prodded with a fork, about 1 hour. Serve hot or warm.

Left, a simple chapel is a destination for religious pilgrimage. Center, horses are ridden on pilgrimages in the countryside. Right, colorful chapels can be found throughout the area.

GRILLED VEGETABLES *with* FRESH HERBS
SERVES 4

Choose vegetables to grill that take about the same amount of time to cook. For example, hard, dense vegetables such as carrots are best matched with wedges of yellow onion, cauliflower and broccoli florets, and slices of Japanese eggplant. The goal is to cook the vegetables until lightly browned and for all of them to be removed from the grill at the same time. If this is going to be a side dish for grilled steaks or chicken, cook the meat first. It can "rest" off the heat without any deterioration of quality for the few minutes it takes to cook the vegetables.

2 red bell peppers

2 yellow bell peppers

2 medium zucchini

2 large portobello mushrooms

1 bunch asparagus

1 teaspoon finely grated orange zest

¼ cup freshly squeezed orange juice

¼ cup thin soy sauce

½ cup extra-virgin olive oil
or unsalted butter

4 cloves garlic, minced

½ teaspoon salt

¼ teaspoon freshly ground black pepper

¼ cup chopped fresh cilantro,
leaves and tender stems

4 limes, cut into wedges

Prepare a medium-hot fire in a gas or charcoal grill.

Cut the bell peppers into wide strips and remove the stems and seeds. Cut each zucchini into 3 long slices. Cut off and discard the mushroom stems, then cut the mushrooms into quarters. Snap off and discard the tough ends of the asparagus stems.

In a medium saucepan, combine the orange zest and juice, soy sauce, olive oil, garlic, salt, pepper, and cilantro. Bring to a simmer and then remove from the heat. This can be done up to 8 hours ahead and kept refrigerated in an airtight container. If made ahead, bring the orange juice mixture back to a simmer.

Brush the grill (or a barbecue grate screen) with oil. Add the vegetables. Brush generously with the herb butter. Grill the vegetables until lightly browned, about 6 minutes, turning them often (ask for a volunteer to help!) and brushing with more herb sauce. Serve with lime wedges on the side.

GRILLED WHITE CORN BRUSHED
with HERB BUTTER

SERVES 4

We wait to make this dish until the summer arrives, bringing with it corn so tender that it can be eaten raw. This herb butter is also delicious brushed on asparagus, mushrooms, or a mix of vegetables about to go on the grill.

HERB BUTTER

4 cloves garlic, peeled

1 serrano chile (optional)

¼ cup packed fresh cilantro, leaves and tender stems

¼ cup packed fresh mint leaves

8 tablespoons unsalted butter, cut into 8 pieces, at room temperature

Finely grated zest of 2 limes

1 teaspoon salt

∽

8 ears white corn, shucked

2 limes, cut into wedges

To make the herb butter, mince the garlic in a food processor. Add the serrano chile, if using, and mince. Add the cilantro and mint and mince again. Add the butter, lime zest, and salt to the food processor. Run the machine until the mixture becomes smooth. This can be done up to 24 hours ahead; refrigerate the butter in an airtight container.

Prepare a medium-hot fire in a gas or charcoal grill. Place the herb butter in a small saucepan over low heat, and heat until the butter melts. Place the corn on a baking pan. Add half of the herb butter, and roll the corn in the butter. Transfer the corn to the grill. As the corn cooks, brush with the leftover butter in the pan. When the corn browns slightly on all sides, remove from the grill. Serve with the lime wedges.

ROASTED VEGETABLES

SERVES 4

Roasted vegetables are easy to make and so satisfying as an accompaniment to meat and seafood dishes. Choose vegetables that are equally dense. Potatoes, parsnips, and carrots have the same degree of firmness. But if you add summer squash, for example, the squash would cook much quicker than the potatoes. A good combination with summer squash would be summer bell pepper strips of various colors, whole green onions, asparagus, and white corn still on the cob.

2 medium russet potatoes

2 large parsnips

4 large carrots

2 medium yellow onions

⅓ cup extra-virgin olive oil

4 cloves garlic, chopped

½ teaspoon ground cinnamon, cumin, or coriander (optional)

½ teaspoon crushed red pepper

Salt and freshly ground black pepper

Preheat the oven to 425°F. Spread a baking sheet with aluminum foil and spray the foil with nonstick cooking spray.

Peel the potatoes and cut in half lengthwise. Cut each half into 3 long strips. Peel the parsnips and carrots, and then trim away the stem area. Cut in half lengthwise. Cut each half on a sharp diagonal into big chunky pieces. Peel the onion. Cut the onions into 8 wedges.

In a large bowl, combine all of the prepared vegetables with the oil, garlic, cinnamon, if using, crushed red pepper, and salt and black pepper to taste. Toss to evenly coat the vegetables with the seasonings and olive oil. Spread on the prepared baking sheet. Place the vegetables in the oven. Roast until tender and golden, about 1 hour, turning the vegetables over twice during the cooking time. Serve hot or at room temperature.

Chapter 10

DESSERTS
to Win Friends

CHOCOLATE–GRAND MARNIER SAUCE
with ANCHO CHILE

MAKES 2 CUPS

Valrhona cocoa powder is densely black and intensely flavored. A few tablespoons of Valrhona cocoa powder added to any chocolate dessert makes a dramatic flavor improvement. Look for its pitch black box at gourmet shops, fancy markets, or order it from www.valrhona.com. This is delicious served over ice cream.

4 ounces bittersweet chocolate

¾ cup heavy cream

4 tablespoons unsalted butter, cut into pieces, at room temperature

¼ cup Valrhona cocoa powder

¼ cup Grand Marnier

1 teaspoon vanilla bean paste or pure vanilla extract

¼ teaspoon ancho chile powder (optional)

Chop the chocolate into very fine pieces. Transfer to a small heatproof bowl. Add the cream, butter pieces, cocoa powder, Grand Marnier, vanilla, and chile powder, if using. Bring 4 inches of water to a rapid boil in a saucepan slightly smaller than the heatproof bowl. Decrease the heat to the lowest setting. Place the bowl over the saucepan so it fits securely but doesn't touch the water. Heat the mixture, stirring occasionally, until all the chocolate melts and the sauce is evenly mixed. Transfer to an airtight container and refrigerate for up to 1 month. To serve, warm the sauce in the microwave oven on high, stirring the sauce every 20 seconds, until melted.

There is a rich tradition of papier-mâché masks, dolls, and decorations for fiestas.

STRAWBERRY COULIS

MAKES 3 CUPS

Coulis refers to a category of thick pureed sauces, sweet or savory. Even a puree of shellfish soup can be called a coulis. The strawberries must be ripe for this recipe, meaning bright red throughout the berry. Don't use any strawberries having a white center. When fresh strawberries are not in season, substitute one 12-ounce bag frozen strawberries with no sugar added. Use the coulis as a sauce on ice cream, cakes, brownies, and to dip cookies into!

1 pint fresh strawberries
or any other berry

½ cup dry red wine

¼ cup sugar

Combine all of the ingredients in a blender and liquefy. Transfer to a small airtight container and store in the refrigerator for up to 5 days.

Pictured clockwise from top: Raspberry-Cabernet Sauvignon Sauce, Caramel Butter Sauce, and Chocolate Caramel Sauce.

RASPBERRY—CABERNET SAUVIGNON SAUCE

MAKES 3 CUPS

This is an intensely flavored and brilliantly colored sauce. It calls for an entire bottle of red wine. We always buy one from the province of "cheap." Be sure to use only a medium-mesh sieve, not a fine-mesh one, to strain the sauce so that everything except the raspberry seeds goes through the sieve. We've also made this using frozen mixed berries in place of the frozen raspberries. The sauce is great on pancakes or waffles, added to a vinaigrette dressing, or brushed on pork tenderloin or butterflied leg of lamb just before taking them off the grill. It also tastes great as a topping for virtually any dessert.

1 (750-milliliter) bottle inexpensive Cabernet Sauvignon or Zinfandel

12 ounces frozen raspberries

1 cup sugar

½ teaspoon freshly ground black pepper

Combine all of the ingredients in a nonreactive 12-inch sauté pan (it doesn't matter if the raspberries are still frozen). Bring to a boil over medium-high heat. Continue to boil for about 15 minutes until reduced to 3½ cups. Remove from the heat and let cool to room temperature. Pour into a blender and liquefy. Pour through a medium-mesh sieve to remove the seeds. Transfer the sauce to a small airtight container and store in the refrigerator for up to 6 months.

CHOCOLATE CARAMEL SAUCE

MAKES 2½ CUPS

This combines two of our favorite dessert sauces. The result is an intense chocolate sauce with the deep underlying flavor of caramel.

1½ cups Caramel Butter
Sauce (recipe follows)

4 ounces bittersweet chocolate

Reheat the caramel sauce if necessary. Chop the chocolate into very fine pieces. Stir into the hot caramel sauce until all the chocolate melts. Transfer to a jar and store in the refrigerator for up to 3 months. To serve, warm the sauce in the microwave on High, stirring every 20 seconds, until melted.

CARAMEL BUTTER SAUCE

MAKES 1½ CUPS

This quick-to-make sauce is somewhat technically difficult because it has to be cooked for just the right amount of time. If cooked for too long, the caramel will taste burned, and if not cooked enough, it will have a gritty sugar-crystal texture. Practice making this a few times in advance of serving it to guests. Then, you'll have plenty of caramel sauce to pour over ice cream, night after night.

1 cup sugar

½ cup heavy cream

2 tablespoons unsalted butter

Place the sugar in a small, heavy stainless-steel saucepan. Place over medium-high heat. When the sugar turns dark brown around the sides of the saucepan, stir the mixture with a wooden spoon or whisk. Cook until the sugar turns a very dark brown and just begins to smoke. Immediately remove the saucepan from the heat. Using a long-handled whisk, slowly stir in the cream, adding it in a continuous stream. The caramel will bubble furiously, so be careful. Stir in the butter. Let cool slightly, then pour into a jar and refrigerate for up to 3 months. To serve, warm the sauce in the microwave on High, stirring the sauce every 20 seconds, until melted.

ROASTED BANANA ICE CREAM
with CARAMEL SAUCE

SERVES 6 TO 10, OR ABOUT 3 PINTS

Roasting bananas heightens their flavor and forms the perfect match with generous servings of homemade caramel sauce. The ice cream is also delicious served with chocolate sauce.

4 ripe bananas, peeled

½ cup lightly packed light brown sugar

1 tablespoon unsalted butter, melted

4 cups heavy cream

1 tablespoon freshly squeezed lemon juice

2 cups granulated sugar

1 teaspoon vanilla bean paste
or pure vanilla extract

½ teaspoon ground cinnamon,
preferably Mexican

¼ teaspoon salt

Caramel Sauce (page 167),
warmed, for serving

Preheat the oven to 400°F. Cut the bananas into ½-inch slices. In a 2-quart baking dish, toss the bananas with the brown sugar and butter. Bake for 40 minutes, stirring once. The bananas should be brown. Let cool before proceeding.

Transfer the bananas to a blender. Add the cream, lemon juice, granulated sugar, vanilla, cinnamon, and salt. Blend to liquefy, but don't let the blender run for more than 10 seconds or it will start to turn the cream to butter. Transfer to an ice cream maker and process according to the manufacturer's instructions. Transfer to a freezer-safe container. Press plastic wrap directly across the surface of the ice cream. Store in the freezer for up to 2 months.

Serve with plenty of warm caramel sauce.

These mohigangas, or large papier-mâché figures, dance to a mariachi band at a birthday party.

COCONUT ICE CREAM

SERVES 6 TO 10, OR ABOUT 2 QUARTS

This rich coconut ice cream is a very refreshing dessert, especially after enjoying spicy Mexican food. Unlike egg-based ice cream, which within a few weeks crystallizes and acquires a stale taste, this ice cream, if properly sealed in a container with plastic wrap pressed across the surface, maintains its perfect flavor for months in the freezer. Serve with any one of the various dessert sauces in this chapter.

3 cups canned unsweetened coconut milk (see page 10)

1½ cups heavy cream

1½ cups sugar

1 cup shredded sweetened coconut

Fresh strawberries or a combination of mixed fresh berries, for serving

Combine the coconut milk, cream, and sugar in a bowl. Transfer to an ice cream machine and process according to the manufacturer's instructions. Transfer to a freezer-safe container. Press plastic wrap directly across the surface. Store in the freezer for up to 2 months. Toast the shredded coconut over low heat until golden, 5 minutes. Cool, transfer to a resealable plastic bag, and freeze for up to 4 months. Serve with one of the sauces from this chapter, a sprinkling of toasted coconut, and garnish with the berries.

CHOCOLATE CHIP–COCONUT COOKIES

MAKES 15 TO 20 COOKIES

There can never be too many chocolate chips in the recipe—or in your hand. When buying them, make sure the bag says "pure" or "real" chocolate chips. A better taste choice and a bit more work is to substitute a good-quality bittersweet chocolate bar such as Valrhona, and to "chip" it into little fragments.

1 cup sweetened shredded coconut

8 tablespoons unsalted butter, at room temperature

½ cup lightly packed light brown sugar

¼ cup granulated sugar

1 large egg

1 teaspoon vanilla bean paste or pure vanilla extract

¾ teaspoon baking powder

½ teaspoon baking soda

¼ teaspoon salt

10 ounces white or dark chocolate chips

1 cup unbleached all-purpose flour

Preheat the oven to 350°F. Grease a baking sheet or line it with parchment paper. Toast the coconut in a dry skillet over low heat until golden, 5 minutes. Remove from the heat and let cool.

In a food processor, combine the butter and sugars. Pulse the machine until the butter and sugars form a ball. Add the egg, vanilla, baking powder, baking soda, and salt. Pulse the food processor a few more times in order to evenly mix everything. Transfer the mixture to a large bowl. Add the toasted coconut and chocolate chips, then stir again. Add the flour in batches, one-third at a time, mixing thoroughly after each addition. The recipe can be completed up to this point and the batter refrigerated for 1 week or frozen for 3 months.

Scoop out the cookie dough 2 tablespoons at a time, and place 1 inch apart on the baking sheet. Bake until light golden, about 12 minutes. Let cool on a rack. The cookies will keep for 3 days at room temperature.

Pictured clockwise from upper left: Horchata (page 186), Hibiscus Tea (page 186), and Chocolate Chip–Coconut Cookies.

MEXICAN CHOCOLATE BROWNIES
with CAYENNE AND CINNAMON

MAKES 12 BROWNIES

This brownie recipe is given a Mexican slant by adding vanilla bean paste, cayenne pepper, and ground cinnamon. The flavor of each of these ingredients perfectly complements the chocolate. The raisins soaked in Jack Daniel's were an addition made by my cooking school assistant, Audreen Maestri, in the early years of the school. It's not authentic Mexican, but the flavor of the Jack Daniel's and the texture of the raisins is the cause for hiding extra brownies for a secret tasting later in the day.

1 cup dark raisins

½ cup Jack Daniel's

¾ cup unsalted butter

8 ounces bittersweet chocolate, finely chopped

3 large eggs

¾ cup granulated sugar

½ cup lightly packed light brown sugar

2 teaspoons vanilla bean paste or pure vanilla extract

½ teaspoon ground cayenne pepper

½ teaspoon ground cinnamon, preferably Mexican

1 cup unbleached all-purpose flour

½ cup toasted walnuts, pecans, or hazelnuts

Vanilla bean ice cream, for serving

Preheat the oven to 350°F. Grease and flour a 9-inch round baking pan or a square glass baking dish. Place the raisins in a small bowl and add the Jack Daniel's. Let soak for 2 hours.

Cut the butter and chocolate into small pieces. Place the butter and chocolate in a heatproof bowl that fits securely over a saucepan with a couple of inches of water. The bowl should not be touching the water. Simmer over low heat, stirring, until the chocolate melts. Remove from the heat and let cool.

Beat the eggs vigorously with a whisk in a large bowl. Stir in the melted chocolate and then the sugars. Stir in the vanilla, cayenne, and cinnamon. Add the raisins and Jack Daniel's to the chocolate mixture. Stir in the flour and nuts. Mix evenly.

Pour the mixture into the prepared pan and bake until just set, about 25 minutes. Let cool in the pan. Turn out of the pan and cut into wedges or squares. The brownies will keep refrigerated for 3 days in an airtight container. Serve at room temperature with ice cream.

CHOCOLATE FUDGE TART *with* HINTS OF CHILE

SERVES 8 TO 12

This recipe takes a European chocolate tart and transforms it by adding favorite Mexican seasonings of orange, cinnamon, and ancho or chipotle chile powder. We like to make it a day in advance and then cut and place it on dessert plates just before guests arrive. With the plates hidden away, for example in the laundry room, it's a simple matter to exchange empty dinner plates for this beautiful chocolate tart, garnished at the last minute with fresh berries and vanilla bean ice cream. Be aware that this tart uses raw eggs.

7 ounces gingersnaps, graham crackers, or plain biscotti

8 tablespoons unsalted butter

10 ounces bittersweet chocolate, finely chopped

1 cup heavy cream

2 teaspoons vanilla bean paste or pure vanilla extract

2 teaspoons finely grated orange zest

½ teaspoon ground cinnamon, preferably Mexican

½ teaspoon ancho or chipotle chile powder

1 large egg

2 egg yolks

Vanilla bean ice cream, for serving

Fresh berries of your choice, for serving

Preheat the oven to 400°F. In a food processor, powder the gingersnaps. Melt the butter. Pour half the butter down the feeder tube with the machine running. Add only enough butter so that the mixture feels crumbly but slightly damp. If the mixture feels dry, then add a little more of the melted butter. Press the gingersnaps across the bottom of a 9- to 10-inch tart pan or springform pan. Bake for 10 minutes, then let cool on a rack.

Place the chocolate in a heatproof bowl and add the cream, vanilla, orange zest, cinnamon, and chile powder. Place the bowl inside a saucepan filled with a few inches of boiling water. The bowl should fit securely in the pan but not be touching the water. Simmer over low heat, stirring, until melted. Remove the bowl from the saucepan. Using a whisk, beat the egg with the egg yolks for 30 seconds, then using the whisk stir this into the chocolate mixture. Pour into the tart pan. Refrigerate until thoroughly chilled. The tart can be made 24 hours ahead and refrigerated.

To serve, cut the tart into wedges and transfer to serving plates. The wedges can be left at room temperature for 2 hours, or the plates refrigerated. Accompany with scoops of ice cream and fresh berries.

FLAN *with* CINNAMON ACCENTS

MAKES TWELVE 4-OUNCE RAMEKINS

This wonderful flan is based on a recipe that San Miguel pastry chef Paco Cardenas taught our cooking class. You can make the flan 24 hours in advance, and then unmold it before dinner guests arrive. Serve it chilled, by itself or with fresh berries.

1½ cups sugar

6 ounces cream cheese, cut into 6 pieces, at room temperature

2 cups whole milk

1 cup condensed milk

6 large eggs

2 teaspoons vanilla bean paste or pure vanilla extract

½ teaspoon ground cinnamon, preferably Mexican

¼ teaspoon salt

Fresh berries and/or raspberries or strawberries (optional)

Preheat the oven to 350°F. Place the sugar in a heavy saucepan over medium heat. Do not stir the sugar. Heat until the sugar turns a caramel color around the edges of the saucepan. Then stir the sugar. Continue stirring until all the sugar melts and turns a caramel color without any grainy texture. Pour the sauce into the bottoms of twelve 4-ounce ramekins. Chill in the freezer for 15 minutes.

In a blender, place the cream cheese, milk, condensed milk, eggs, vanilla, cinnamon, and salt. Puree until liquefied. Pour into the ramekins.

Place the ramekins in a roasting pan, and carefully add hot tap water to a depth of 1 inch. Transfer the roasting pan to the oven, and bake the flans for 40 to 45 minutes. They are done when you gently shake a ramekin and the custard does not wobble. Remove the pan from the oven. When cool enough to handle, remove the ramekins from the water bath. Then refrigerate for at least 4 hours or up to 24 hours.

To serve, run a paring knife around the inside of each ramekin to help loosen the flan. Pour 1 inch of water into a 12-inch frying pan. Bring to a boil, then turn off the heat. Dip each ramekin into the water for 15 seconds to loosen the flan. Then invert onto a serving plate. This can be done 24 hours in advance of serving, with the flans kept refrigerated. Just before serving, add fresh berries outside of each ramekin.

GINGER ICE CREAM

MAKES 2 QUARTS

This is a refreshing ice cream—a perfect conclusion following a complex-tasting Mexican meal. You'll find ginger liqueur at higher-end and larger liquor stores. The most common brand is Domaine de Canton. The ice cream may take a little longer to freeze with the addition of the liqueur, so be patient. Even without the liqueur, the ice cream has a very nice ginger flavor.

1 (6-inch) piece fresh ginger

2 cups whole milk

4 cups heavy cream

1 cup ginger liqueur (optional)

1½ cups sugar

Peel the ginger and cut it crosswise into paper-thin slices. Transfer the slices to a food processor or mini chopper and mince. You will need 1 cup of minced ginger. Place the ginger and milk in a blender. Blend until liquefied.

Transfer to a large saucepan and add 2 cups of the cream. Bring to a simmer over low heat. Immediately remove from the heat and let rest at room temperature for 30 minutes. Then strain the ginger cream through a medium-mesh sieve into a large bowl. Discard the solids.

Add the remaining 2 cups cream, liqueur, if using, and sugar to the bowl. Stir to evenly combine. Process in an ice cream maker according to the manufacturer's instructions. Transfer to a freezer-safe container. Press plastic wrap directly across the surface. Store in the freezer for up to 2 months.

Around Easter, traditional handicrafts are used for decorations, such as these sugar-sculpture chickens and delicate candles.

FALLEN KAHLÚA CHOCOLATE CAKE
with STRAWBERRY COULIS

SERVES 12

This recipe has three of our favorite ingredients: Kahlúa, Valrhona cocoa powder, and vanilla bean paste. Kahlúa is a rum and coffee liqueur from the high mountains of Veracruz. It is a blend of pure sugarcane and rum with enticing flavor notes of vanilla and caramel. Valrhona cocoa powder is black and intensely chocolaty. If you can't find this, it can be ordered at www.valrhona.com. Vanilla bean paste is a thick syrup filled with specks of vanilla bean. It's more complex-tasting than vanilla extract. For recipes using vanilla extract, substitute the same amount of vanilla bean paste.

8 tablespoons unsalted butter, at room temperature

1 cup sugar

2 large eggs

¼ cup Valrhona or Guittard cocoa powder

1 tablespoon vanilla bean paste or pure vanilla extract

½ teaspoon baking soda

½ teaspoon baking powder

½ teaspoon ground cinnamon, preferably Mexican

½ teaspoon ancho chile powder

¼ teaspoon salt

½ cup Kahlúa

¾ cup plus 2 tablespoons unbleached all-purpose flour

Strawberry Coulis (page 165)

1 pint fresh strawberries, stemmed and halved

Preheat the oven to 350°F. Line an 8-inch springform pan with parchment paper. Cut the butter into 8 pieces. In a food processor or an electric mixer fitted with a balloon whisk, place the butter and sugar. Process or mix until the butter has absorbed all of the sugar and has become soft and fluffy (the butter-sugar mixture will have formed into a ball).

With the food processor or mixer running, add the eggs one at a time. When evenly combined, add the cocoa powder and combine. Add the vanilla, baking soda, baking powder, cinnamon, chile powder, and salt. Process or mix until very smooth. With the machine running, add the Kahlúa. When evenly combined, transfer the chocolate mixture to a large bowl. Add the flour, and stir the chocolate batter with a whisk until smooth.

Pour the batter into the prepared pan. Place the pan on a baking sheet, and bake until the cake no longer moves when you jiggle the baking pan, about 30 minutes. Do not overcook or the center will not "fall"! Let cool on a rack. The cake can be prepared up to this point 24 hours in advance and refrigerated. When cool, the Kahlúa cake should have "fallen" in the center.

To serve, before dinner bring to room temperature. Slice the cake and place on serving plates. When ready to serve, surround each slice with the strawberry coulis and halved strawberries.

MEXICAN CHOCOLATE TRUFFLES

MAKES 16 TRUFFLES

Now a different type of feast draws to a close. The recipe for Gravlox Infused with Chiles, Cilantro, and Tequila opened the appetizer chapter and welcomed you to our love of Mexican flavors and entertaining, and these delicious chocolate truffles serve as our fond farewell. Gather around the table to celebrate the triumph of Mexican food, both traditional and contemporary. Then gather again. Let's celebrate.

The combination of vanilla, grated orange zest, and ancho chile powder gives these chocolate truffles a Mexican taste. Serve them as the main dessert with fresh berries, or as a chocolate accent to a non-chocolate dessert such as flan. They are also delicious with vanilla bean ice cream or Coconut Ice Cream (page 169). For maximum flavor impact, make these with a great bittersweet chocolate, such as Scharffen Berger, Valrhona, Dagoba, or Green & Black's.

8 ounces bittersweet chocolate

½ cup heavy cream

2 tablespoons unsweetened cocoa powder

2 tablespoons sugar

2 teaspoons vanilla bean paste
or pure vanilla extract

2 teaspoons finely grated orange zest

1 teaspoon ancho chile powder

1 cup pecans or hazelnuts

Cut the chocolate into very fine slices or shards. In a small heatproof bowl, combine the chocolate, cream, cocoa powder, sugar, vanilla, orange zest, and ancho chile powder. Place the bowl over a saucepan of barely simmering water so that it fits snugly. The bowl should not touch the simmering water. Turn off the heat. With a whisk, stir the chocolate mixture until all the chocolate has melted and the mixture is combined. Spread the chocolate mixture evenly across a dinner plate. Place in the refrigerator until the mixture becomes very firm, about 30 minutes.

Meanwhile, preheat the oven to 350°F. Toast the nuts on a baking sheet until they darken slightly, about 15 minutes. Let cool to room temperature. If using hazelnuts, wrap them in a clean kitchen towel and rub vigorously to remove the brown skins. Place the nuts in a food processor and finely chop.

When the chocolate mixture becomes firm, use a dessert spoon to separate the chocolate into 12 to 16 equal-size pieces. Roll each piece between your palms into a ball. Then roll the chocolate balls in the chopped nuts. Place on a clean plate and refrigerate. The truffles can be stored for 5 days in the refrigerator in an airtight container. Be sure to bring to room temperature before serving.

Clockwise from top left: A balloon vendor in the town center. Easter candles emphasize the spring season. A flute player participates in a neighborhood festival. A local fountain decorated by a group of neighbors before Easter.

Chapter 11

DRINKS
to Refresh and Elevate the Spirit

Tequila

Lick the back of the hand between finger and thumb and add a sprinkle of salt. Without pause, lick the salt, sip the tequila, and finish by biting into a lime slice. With no hesitation—repeat. That is a typical introduction to tequila, gringo style, in Cabo San Lucas. Not much else remembered.

Tequila is Mexico's national drink. It is distilled from blue agave plants that grow around the city of Tequila and in the highlands of the western Mexican state of Jalisco. More than 300 million blue agave are harvested each year to satisfy the national thirst for tequila's sophisticated flavor. Tequila was first produced in the fifteenth century near the city of Tequila. When the conquistadors ran out of their own brandy, they began to distill agave. Most tequila brands today are owned by large multinational corporations. However, there are more than 100 distilleries making 900 marketed brands.

There are four primary categories of tequila.

BLANCO ("WHITE") OR PLATA ("SILVER") is aged less than 2 months in stainless-steel tanks or neutral oak barrels. This is the type typically used for mixed drinks such as margaritas.

REPOSADO ("RESTED") is aged for a minimum of 2 months but less than 1 year in oak barrels of any size. The bottle should always say "100% Agave Reposado."

AÑEJO ("AGED") OR ("VINTAGE") is aged for a minimum of 1 year but less than 3 years in small oak barrels. Many of the barrels are from whiskey distilleries in the United States or Canada. Jack Daniel's barrels are a favored type.

EXTRA AÑEJO ("EXTRA AGED") OR ("ULTRA AGED") is aged for a minimum of 3 years in oak barrels.

Always store reposado and añejo in the freezer. This is true for mezcal, too. Serve reposado and añejo, chilled, at the end of dinner parties in tequila glasses or sake cups. Enjoy the many levels of flavor of reposado and añejo sipped neat. Or, alternate with sips of Sangrita (page 190). Good tequila is never served on the rocks.

When cooking, we've used silver tequila to cure salmon, such as in the Gravlax Infused with Chiles, Cilantro, and Tequila (page 34). But tequila is an excellent addition in any cold dish, such as a jigger added to salsa, or to Serrano Gazpacho (page 89), or to Chilled Avocado Soup (page 94).

Mezcal

Mezcal is distilled from the maguey plant, a form of agave. Maguey, of which there are more than 120 subspecies, grows in many parts of Mexico, but most mezcal is made in the state of Oaxaca. There are about 330,000 hectares cultivated for maguey, owned by 9,000 producers. Over 6 million liters of mezcal are produced in Mexico annually, with more than 150 brand names. Mezcal is consumed straight and never as part of a cocktail mix. It has a strong smoky flavor, which is one of the reasons it has not become as popular as tequila. Mezcal is exported, but mostly to the United States and Japan.

To make mezcal, the heart of the agave is smoked in earthen mounds over pits of hot rocks. Mezcal is highly varied because of the range of fruits and herbs added during fermentation. Most mezcal falls into the same categories as tequila: blanco, reposado, and añejo. The stories about the best bottles of mezcal always containing a worm are unfounded. If present, this is the larva of a moth that infests maguey plants. It's added during bottling as a marketing tool. The worm is no indication of the quality of the mezcal. Experiment and serve both a tequila and a mezcal, icy cold, at the end of a dinner. Taste, compare, and discuss. Use this as impetus to plan the group's next Mexican-inspired dinner.

Chef Juan Carlos Escalante's Drinks, page 190

In San Miguel, the value of a property is measured by its view of a great sunset.

Beer

Beer is the ideal drink for the whole range of Mexican food, from taco stands to refined Mexico City restaurants. It's a low-alcohol drink with a refreshing hops flavor that balances the complex range of flavors of chiles, cilantro, lime, and sweetness. It's the perfect flavor complement to the rich mole sauces on pages 122–125, BBQ Sea Bass Tacos (page 56), and Chiles Rellenos (page 59). Take a sip of Serrano Gazpacho (page 89), or bite into BBQ Shrimp Packed with Serrano-Herb Butter (page 42), then take a sip of beer, and the palate is immediately refreshed and ready for the next bite. Even if you are serving wine, experiment with Mexican beer, too. Offer a choice of dark and light Mexican beers, and be sure to serve them icy cold. And, if you wish, accompany the beer with slices or wedges of lime, a custom not common in Mexico.

Wine

Down a dusty road we ventured in August 2006, driving the length of Guadalupe Valley, the premier wine-making region of Mexico, located in Baja California. There were no road signs, and an occasional winery appeared in the distance. There were no crowds, but it was a charming little vacation to put to rest grandiose descriptions of "the next Napa Valley." The arrival sequence was enchanting. Adobe Guadalupe was a lovely winery with an attached deluxe inn, complete with a Swiss chef and great food. We were graciously welcomed by owner Don Miller, and before long we gathered in the tasting room, hearing Don's story (impassioned, charismatic, insightful, funny) about his move from Orange County and the development of the winery. First we tasted Uriel, a rosé of Cabernet Franc, Tempranillo, Grenache, Chenin Blanc, Muscatel, Viognier, and Syrah—low in alcohol, bone dry, highly acidic, extremely refreshing, and as good as any Napa Valley rosé. Next was Gabriel 2003, a red wine blend of 70 percent Merlot, 23 percent Cabernet Sauvignon, and 7 percent Malbec. Hugh's tasting notes read, "high acid, nice fruit, balanced, long finish, 13.9%, wonderful."

Thus began a reckoning with prejudice. Up and down the valley we traveled with Don Miller, in and out of wineries large and small. Everywhere there were owners to meet, wines to taste, and plans for return visits.

In Guadalupe Valley, fifty wineries produce 90 percent of Mexico's wine. Baja's humid winters, dry warm summer days, and cool evening sea breezes that flow up the valley as it gains elevation all provide a good growing environment. The reason we're unfamiliar with Mexican wines is because the Mexican government imposes a 40 percent tax on wine in order to protect their beer and tequila industries. This tax makes Mexican wines too expensive for the export market. But we do our own personal importing. We never return from San Miguel without an extra suitcase filled with bottles of Mexican wine.

Most Mexican wines are sold in Mexico City, Monterrey, Guadalajara, Puebla, and in the tourist areas such as Cancun and Cabo San Lucas. La Laguna, the oldest wine-making region in Mexico, straddles the state of Coahuila and Durango. The Parras Valley rises to 1,500 meters and has a perfect mix of warm days, cool nights, and low humidity. The most important winery is Casa Madero, which also happens to be the oldest winery in the New World. It is famous for its outstanding Chardonnay and Syrah.

A newly sprouted wine region is in central Mexico around the cities of Zacatecas and Queretaro, where wine-making is still in its infancy.

The development of great wines from Mexico is the result of the brilliant vision and boundless energy of one man, Hugo D'Acosta. He is the George Washington of Baja wines. Not only is he the consulting winemaker for many of the key Baja wineries, but he also runs a school of enology that attracts students from throughout Mexico. In addition, he and his wife, Gloria, started their own winery in 1997, Casa de Piedra. They produce a white called Piedra del Sol, an unoaked Chardonnay, and a red Vino de Piedra, which is 50 percent Cabernet and 50 percent Tempranillo. No drive is too long to taste these great wines!

WINES TO SERVE WITH THESE RECIPES
Matching the proper wine with food accents the special flavors of both and brings to the foreground understated, alluring flavors. Many of this book's assertive flavors will overwhelm the subtlety of a fine white or red wine. For example, a dish such as Roast Rack of Lamb with Coffee, Chiles, and Chocolate (page 142), with its generous use of chile, will exaggerate the tannins in red wine and ruin the wine. For the appetizers, salads, soups, and seafood main courses, serve Sauvignon Blanc, Pinot Grigio, dry Riesling, dry Gewürztraminer, and French Chenin Blanc. For the meat main dishes, good choices are Zinfandel, Pinot Noir, and Merlot. Taste, discuss, compare, and then begin planning a wine-buying trip to Baja's Guadalupe Valley.

HIBISCUS TEA (JAMAICA)

MAKES 8 CUPS

Hibiscus water has a floral, tropical, tart flavor with a striking red intensity. We first tasted this at Rancho de la Capilla, located just outside of San Miguel. This refreshing chilled drink is great enjoyed on its own or to accompany any of the recipes in this book.

8 cups water

½ cup dried hibiscus flowers

¾ cup sugar

Bring the water to a boil in a saucepan. Remove from the heat, and stir in the hibiscus. Let soak for 30 minutes. Pour through a mesh sieve to remove the flowers. Stir in the sugar. Taste and add more sugar if desired. Chill before serving. This will keep, refrigerated, for 1 week.

HORCHATA

MAKES 5 CUPS

This is a rice drink common throughout Mexico. But horchata is rarely served north of the border except at Mexican restaurants located in Mexican communities. Steve Zazula and Kathy Lichter, owners of Rancho de la Capilla near San Miguel de Allende, have made this many times for our groups. Any of the following types of white rice are equally good: California or Texas long-grain, basmati, or Thai jasmine. Adding 1 to 2 teaspoons vanilla extract, or "fortifying" the horchata with a little chilled tequila, is a nice variation. Serve this as a refreshing drink on its own or with any of the appetizers in this book.

1½ cups long-grain white rice

6 cups cold water

1 (5-ounce) can evaporated milk

¼ cup sweetened condensed milk

¼ teaspoon ground cinnamon, preferably Mexican

4 to 6 fresh strawberries, sliced

Mint sprigs, for garnish

In a large bowl, soak the rice in the cold water for 2 hours.

Combine both milks and the cinnamon with the rice and water mixture. Process in batches in a blender for 2 minutes on the highest speed. Taste, and if you prefer the drink sweeter, add more condensed milk and blend again. Pour through a fine-mesh sieve, and discard the solids. Refrigerate for at least 2 hours before serving. You will notice that the chalky solids settle to the bottom. Carefully pour the liquid into another container, stopping when you reach the solids. This will keep, refrigerated, for 5 days.

When ready to serve, transfer to a pitcher and add the strawberries. Pour into glasses filled with ice cubes and garnish each glass with a mint sprig.

CUCUMBER TEA

MAKES 8 CUPS

This is a wonderfully refreshing tea provided you make it at least a day in advance of serving. The taste on the first day is forgettable, so be patient! And don't be tempted to add any sugar. The drink acquires a beautiful natural sweetness from the cucumber on the second day.

1 hothouse cucumber, or 3 Japanese or Middle Eastern cucumbers

4 mint sprigs, plus more for garnish

1 or more whole small dried chiles, not seeded (optional)

8 cups cold water

Cut enough of the cucumber into approximately ½ by ½-inch cubes to fill 2 cups (or thinly slice the cucumber). The cucumber does not have to be peeled or seeded. Combine the cucumber, mint, dried chile, if using, and water in a large container. Cover and refrigerate overnight before serving. This will keep, refrigerated, for 3 days.

Serve this with the cucumber and a mint sprig in each glass.

FRUIT SMOOTHIES

MAKES 5 CUPS

This brilliantly colored drink requires perfectly ripe strawberries that are a deep red right to the center. We often serve this to welcome guests to a dinner party, presenting it in martini glasses or shot glasses. Substitute other fruits for the berries, individually or in combination, such as mango, papaya, peaches, or nectarines. Apple juice, tonic water, or sparkling wine can be substituted for the orange juice. Add tequila to taste!

1 cup sliced fresh strawberries

1 cup fresh raspberries

1 cup freshly squeezed orange juice

1 cup ice cubes

¼ cup freshly squeezed lime juice

¼ cup or more tequila (optional)

Mint sprigs, for garnish

Combine the berries, orange juice, ice cubes, lime juice, and tequila, if using, in a blender. Blend until smooth. If the puree is too thick, add more orange juice. Pour into 6 martini, highball, or wine glasses. This can be made 24 hours in advance and refrigerated. Stir before serving. Garnish with mint sprigs.

CAFÉ DE OLLA

MAKES 8 CUPS

Olla is the Mexican clay cooking pot used for making stews, mole, rice dishes, and this unique coffee. The coffee is made in a way similar to American boiled camp-style coffee, but with additional flavorings of piloncillo (Mexican sugar), orange slices, and cinnamon sticks.

1 cup freshly ground coffee beans

2 (4-ounce) piloncillo cones or 1 cup lightly packed dark brown sugar

½ orange, cut into ¼-inch slices

2 sticks cinnamon, preferably Mexican

8 cups water

In a large stainless-steel saucepan or a Mexican clay pot (*olla*), combine the ground coffee, sugar, orange slices, cinnamon sticks, and water. Bring to a simmer over medium heat. Cover and simmer for 30 minutes.

Use a slotted spoon to remove the orange slices and discard. Let cool slightly, and then strain through a fine-mesh sieve. Discard the solids. Serve chilled over ice cubes, or hot as a breakfast or after-dinner drink.

Variation

Chop 4 ounces bittersweet chocolate into little pieces, and stir them into the simmering coffee just before serving the coffee hot.

CHEF JUAN CARLOS ESCALANTE'S DRINKS

In the early years of our school, we used to crowd into the tiny kitchen of Juan Carlos Escalante's wonderful Nirvana Restaurant for Monday morning classes. Young, handsome, and talented, he introduced us to many great dishes, including shrimp glazed with hibiscus sauce, pork with achiote, and stuffed chicken with squash blossoms. Then while the restaurant staff set the long dining table, we crowded around Juan Carlos at the bar for these drinks. Another fantastic morning.

LA BANDERA
SERVES 1

This is the classic Mexican way to taste a good-quality tequila. The three colors represent the colors of the Mexican flag (*la bandera*): green, white, and red. Good tequila should be served cold from the freezer.

2 ounces freshly squeezed lime juice

2 ounces tequila (use 100% agave gold or *añejo* quality)

2 ounces Sangrita (recipe follows)

Place the lime juice, tequila, and sangrita into 3 separate glasses. Sip in the order listed; repeat.

SANGRITA
MAKES 2 CUPS

Sangrita or "little blood" is the foundation for many Mexican drinks, including Bloody Marys. You can substitute a spicy tomato juice or a Bloody Mary mix for the tomato juice.

4 ounces freshly squeezed lime juice

2 ounces freshly squeezed orange juice

8 ounces tomato juice

2 tablespoons Worcestershire sauce

1 tablespoon of your favorite hot sauce such as Cholula Brand

1 teaspoon salt

In a small pitcher, combine the juices, Worcestershire, hot sauce, and salt, and stir well. This can be made 3 days in advance of serving. Sip it after each sip of tequila, or serve it by itself, on the rocks.

MEXICAN BLOODY MARY

SERVES 4

For many visitors, this is the wake-up drink for another exciting day in Mexico. But it is also a great welcoming drink for lunch and dinner gatherings.

2 cups Sangrita (page 190)

6 ounces silver tequila

1 stick celery or jicama, cut into 4 long thin pieces

Place the sangrita and tequila in a large cocktail shaker. Add several ice cubes and shake vigorously. Pour into 4 highball glasses filled with ice cubes. Garnish each with a stick of celery.

JUAN CARLOS'S MARGARITA ON THE ROCKS

SERVES 2

If you want a lower-alcohol margarita, add a simple syrup (equal amounts of sugar and water that is brought to a boil, then chilled). Or add 2 ounces of cold water. The margaritas will still be excellent. Jiggers can vary in size, but we use a 2-ounce (¼ cup) amount. Cointreau can be substituted for the triple sec, but remember, Cointreau has a higher alcohol level.

¼ cup kosher salt

1½ ounces freshly squeezed lime juice, plus more for rimming the glass

2 ounces ice-cold silver tequila

2 ounces triple sec

1½ ounces freshly squeezed orange juice

2 slices lime

Scatter the salt evenly across a dessert plate. Run a cut lime around the edge of two glasses. Then dip the edge of the glass into the salt. Fill the margarita glasses with ice cubes. Pour the tequila, triple sec, lime juice, and orange juice into a cocktail shaker filled with ice. Shake vigorously for 10 seconds. Strain equally into both glasses. Alternatively, combine all of the ingredients in a small pitcher, stir well, and then pour into the chilled ice-filled margarita glasses. Place a slice of lime on each rim for garnish.

BLENDED MARGARITAS

SERVES 4

Blended Margaritas most commonly are margaritas and ice mixed into a smooth consistency in an electric blender. Our favorite blended margaritas add fruit such as mango, strawberries, or raspberries. The taste and the color are fantastic.

2 cups (16 ounces) Fruit Smoothies (page 187)

2 ounces silver tequila

2 ounces triple sec

Place the ingredients for the fruit smoothies in an electric blender. Add the tequila and triple sec. Blend until smooth. Pour into martini, highball, or wine glasses. Alternatively, serve the blended mixture on the rocks.

Cool and shady patios invite the guest to enter a home.

ACKNOWLEDGMENTS

Many friends helped bring this book into print and we deeply appreciate their support and many contributions. Thank you, Andrews McMeel Publishing, particularly publisher and president Kirsty Melville, who has been our publisher and editor for ten of our previous cookbooks. Many thanks also to our editor, Jean Lucas, who guided the creation of the book and provided invaluable insights at every step. Thanks also to talented book designer Diane Marsh and art director Tim Lynch.

Carol Cole added her culinary talents to the food styling, and mapmaker Russ Charpentier brought the complicated historical drama of the beginning of the Mexican independence movement to life with his maps of the San Miguel area.

Many people from San Miguel contributed their unique skills. Thank you, Dianne Kushner, for providing us with a beautiful rancho—the home for our cooking school for our first five years, and the scene of many of our cooking school photos. Now due to the generosity of Pedro Guerrero, general manager of Casa de Sierra Nevada, our school is located at their beautiful houseware shop, Sazon. A special thanks to Sierra Nevada chef Emanuel Cervantes for his kindness at the hotel restaurant, Andanza, and at our classes at Sazon. The school in San Miguel would have been impossible without the attention to every detail by two skilled assistants. Many thanks to Audreen Maestri, who was my assistant for five years, and to CC Stark, who is my assistant now. What a pleasure it has been to work with both of you.

Kathy Lichter and Steve Zazula host our rancho cooking classes and lunches at their historic Rancho de la Capilla in an unforgettable setting. Many of the photos of the "Rancho Ladies" cooking, and other stylish photos, were set in the main house of the Rancho de la Capilla. And many of our groups have enjoyed early morning horseback riding through the countryside with Steve. Every "graduation" concludes at the home of jeweler Bill Harris and Howard Haynes. Bill and his great jewelry designer, Luis Pantoja, are always ready to help members of our group choose from their huge selection of fine art jewelry!

A special note of thanks goes to the following artists who enrich the San Miguel program in so many ways: Annemarie and Gary Slipper, Toller Cranston, Dan and Nisha Ferguson, Susan Page and Meyer Schacter,

Merry Calderoni, Juan Ezcurdia, Marion Perlet (we mourn your passing), Fernando Diaz, Anita Middleton (a bright light, gone too soon), Margarette Dawit, David Leonardo, and Ellen Johnson.

The food of San Miguel has been transformed by these talented chefs. Dining at their restaurants has been an important part of our program. Thank you Chef Donnie Masterton at the Restaurant, Chef Juan Carlos Escalante at Nirvana, Chef Cuatepotzo and food and beverage Manager Sebastian Acosta at Restaurant Moxi at Hotel Matilda, owner Max Altamirano at Tio Lucas, Chef Paco Cardenas at El Petit Four, Juan Carlos Cuevas Almazan at Planta Baja, Chef David Jahnke and the owners of MX Restaurant, Arturo Regalado and Paola Millan, and Chef Gonzalo Martinez.

Many others have made invaluable contributions. Thank you to our transport director, Leandro Delgado, to Bill and Heidi LeVasseur at Casa de la Cuesta, and to house rental expert Annie Reutinger, shipper Michael Vidargas, cultural ambassadors Michael and Valerie Coon, guitarists Frances Zelenka and Jack Stillwater, Robert Waters at his B&B, jeweler Joan Vidargas, Patsy Dubois, who conducted classes for us in the early years of our school, and to Theresa Jones, founder of Sazon.

After the recipes were tested at our home and used in cooking classes, the following home cooks gave their final evaluations. This book gained much from their insights. Thank you Susan Anderson, Tom and Tina Barrett, Beth Belden, George Cunningham, Kim and George David, Kathy Dunkle, Marty Flannery, Loren George, Luke George, Bobbie and Richard Handel, Lynne Hood, Geri and Fred Howard, Diane Jackson, Kris Johnson, Bettylu and Lou Kessler, Sandy Lefever, Pat and Laurie Lott, Lynn Maltz, Kim Manthei, Marie Mitchell, Bob and Sanchia Mazza, Ann O'Mara and Wayne Peters, Daliah and Harvey Organ, Sherry Patterson and Don Meldrum, Peg Philleo, Beth Anne Randall, Terre Sisson, Tim and Andrew Wilson, Beth Wisinki, Carol Zimmerman, and Susan Zubik.

An aged bell waits for a new life on a rancho.

METRIC CONVERSIONS
and EQUIVALENTS

Approximate Metric Equivalents

VOLUME

¼ teaspoon	1 milliliter
½ teaspoon	2.5 milliliters
¾ teaspoon	4 milliliters
1 teaspoon	5 milliliters
1¼ teaspoons	6 milliliters
1½ teaspoons	7.5 milliliters
1¾ teaspoons	8.5 milliliters
2 teaspoons	10 milliliters
1 tablespoon (½ fluid ounce)	15 milliliters
2 tablespoons (1 fluid ounce)	30 milliliters
¼ cup	60 milliliters
⅓ cup	80 milliliters
½ cup (4 fluid ounces)	120 milliliters
⅔ cup	160 milliliters
¾ cup	180 milliliters
1 cup (8 fluid ounces)	240 milliliters
1¼ cups	300 milliliters
1½ cups (12 fluid ounces)	360 milliliters
1⅔ cups	400 milliliters
2 cups (1 pint)	460 milliliters
3 cups	700 milliliters
4 cups (1 quart)	0.95 liter
1 quart plus ¼ cup	1 liter
4 quarts (1 gallon)	3.8 liters

WEIGHT

¼ ounce	7 grams
½ ounce	14 grams
¾ ounce	21 grams
1 ounce	28 grams
1¼ ounces	35 grams
1½ ounces	42.5 grams
1⅔ ounces	45 grams
2 ounces	57 grams
3 ounces	85 grams
4 ounces (¼ pound)	113 grams
5 ounces	142 grams
6 ounces	170 grams
7 ounces	198 grams
8 ounces (½ pound)	227 grams
16 ounces (1 pound)	454 grams
35.25 ounces (2.2 pounds)	1 kilogram

LENGTH

⅛ inch	3 millimeters
¼ inch	6 millimeters
½ inch	1¼ centimeters
1 inch	2½ centimeters
2 inches	5 centimeters
2½ inches	6 centimeters
4 inches	10 centimeters
5 inches	13 centimeters
6 inches	15 ¼ centimeters
12 inches (1 foot)	30 centimeters

Metric Conversion Formulas

TO CONVERT	MULTIPLY	TO CONVERT	MULTIPLY
Ounces to grams	Ounces by 28.35	Cups to liters	Cups by .236
Pounds to kilograms	Pounds by .454	Pints to liters	Pints by .473
Teaspoons to milliliters	Teaspoons by 4.93	Quarts to liters	Quarts by .946
Tablespoons to milliliters	Tablespoons by 14.79	Gallons to liters	Gallons by 3.785
Fluid ounces to milliliters	Fluid ounces by 29.57	Inches to centimeters	Inches by 2.54
Cups to milliliters	Cups by 236.59		

Oven Temperatures

To convert Fahrenheit to Celsius, subtract 32 from Fahrenheit, multiply the result by 5, then divide by 9.

DESCRIPTION	FAHRENHEIT	CELSIUS	BRITISH GAS MARK
Very cool	200°	95°	0
Very cool	225°	110°	¼
Very cool	250°	120°	½
Cool	275°	135°	1
Cool	300°	150°	2
Warm	325°	165°	3
Moderate	350°	175°	4
Moderately hot	375°	190°	5
Fairly hot	400°	200°	6
Hot	425°	220°	7
Very hot	450°	230°	8
Very hot	475°	245°	9

Common Ingredients and Their Approximate Equivalents

1 cup uncooked white rice = 185 grams

1 cup all-purpose flour = 140 grams

1 stick butter (4 ounces • ½ cup • 8 tablespoons) = 110 grams

1 cup butter (8 ounces • 2 sticks • 16 tablespoons) = 220 grams

1 cup brown sugar, firmly packed = 225 grams

1 cup granulated sugar = 200 grams

Information compiled from a variety of sources, including *Recipes into Type* by Joan Whitman and Dolores Simon (Newton, MA: Biscuit Books, 2000); *The New Food Lover's Companion* by Sharon Tyler Herbst (Hauppauge, NY: Barron's, 1995); and *Rosemary Brown's Big Kitchen Instruction Book* (Kansas City, MO: Andrews McMeel, 1998).

INDEX

Andrews McMeel Publishing, LLC,
an Andrews McMeel Universal company,
1130 Walnut Street, Kansas City, Missouri 64106.

www.andrewsmcmeel.com

14 15 16 17 18 TEN 10 9 8 7 6 5 4 3 2 1

ISBN: 978-1-4494-5366-4

Library of Congress Control Number: 2014930737

Design: Diane Marsh
Photography: © Teri Sandison 2014
Maps: © Russ Charpentier 2014
Food Stylist: Carol Cole

www.hughcarpenter.com
www.terisandison.com

Front cover: Native Mexican ingredients such as varieties of corn, beans, chiles, tomatillos, squashes, and avocados.

Back cover: The Parroquia church in San Miguel de Allende.

ATTENTION: SCHOOLS AND BUSINESSES

Andrews McMeel books are available at quantity discounts with bulk purchase for educational, business, or sales promotional use. For information, please e-mail the Andrews McMeel Special Sales Department: specialsales@amuniversal.com